Mark Davidson is a chaplain in the Royal Navy. In 2013 he completed a PhD in practical theology, focusing on the moral emotions and disability studies. His primary research interests are pastoral care, community-building and contextual theology.

## To Dr George Gaskin, 4 March 1793

Agamemnon Chatham March 4th 1793

Sir

I have to request that You will have the goodness, to offer my solicitations to the Society for promoting Christian Knowledge, for a donation of Bibles & Prayer book, for the use of the Ships Crew under my Command consisting of 500 men.

I am Sir
With great respect
Your Most Obedient Servant

Horatio Nelson

## To Dr George Gaskin, 26 January 1798

Bath Janr: 26th 1798

Sir

As your Society was so good as to supply me with a quantity of Common Prayers, together with some Religious Tracts to be distributed among the Seamen, when I went out in the Agamemnon in the year 1793, & which I flatter myself answered the good purposes they were intended for.

I have to request the favor that they will order as many Bibles & Prayer Books as may be consistent with their regulations, for the use of such of His Majesty's Ships as I may Hoist my flag in. I am Sir

Your most obliged
Humble Servt:

Horatio Nelson

**Care for souls: Nelson and the SPCK**

# WAR CRIES

## Military prayers from barracks to battlefield

Compiled by the Revd
Dr Mark Davidson RN

First published in Great Britain in 2015

Society for Promoting Christian Knowledge
36 Causton Street
London SW1P 4ST
www.spck.org.uk

*British Library Cataloguing-in-Publication Data*
A catalogue record for this book is available from the British Library

ISBN 978–0–281–07364–1
eBook ISBN 978–0–281–07365–8

Typeset by Graphicraft Limited, Hong Kong
First printed in Great Britain by Ashford Colour Press

eBook by Graphicraft Limited, Hong Kong

Produced on paper from sustainable forests

*For Ellen, Fraser and Sophia*

*Sir, my concern is not whether God is on our side; my greatest concern is to be on God's side, for God is always right.*
Abraham Lincoln

# *Contents*

# Contents

## 2 *Preserve us . . . from the violence of the enemy . . .*

### Prayers for the quarterdeck and airfield    24

## *Contents*

## 3 *You strode before us down that dreadful road . . .*

### Army and Tri-Service prayers

## Contents

## 4  *Smoke clouds enwrap me and cannons are crashing . . .*

### Prayers in the midst of war                                66

# Contents

*Contents*

## 6 *Stretch forth your wounded hands . . .*
### Prayers after the battle

## 7 *Where there is hatred, let me sow love . . .*

### Prayers of reconciliation, return and remembrance

# Contents

# *Foreword*

For people of faith, prayer is an essential activity. As Mark Davidson says, it is in prayer that a Christian engages at a spiritual level. For that reason, a Christian aspires to pray well. But the prayerful know that it is all too easy to let it become banal, routine and mechanical.

Some of the greatest spiritual exemplars are not afraid to admit to the challenges of prayer. It is said that Michael Ramsey, that profoundly prayerful Archbishop of Canterbury, was once asked by a journalist how long he had been praying that morning, 'About five minutes,' came the reply. 'Well, that is not very much for a spiritual leader,' remarked the journalist. 'Yes, but it took me an hour to get there,' was the response. That story may be apocryphal, but it speaks of the human effort to get to the heart of prayer, which is to pray in a way that conforms to the will of God.

This fascinating collection shows the strivings of humanity to do just that. Sometimes the prayers here reflect the time of their composition, or the tradition of the person who composed them. With hindsight, we can see how some do not fit into our current conceptions.

But they show in all the moral complexity of military service a desire to draw close to God and to behave in the best way possible in his service.

In times of demanding service and intense activity, it does no favours to become too complex in what is offered in prayer. This book is a rich resource both for public prayer, but also for more reflective moments. Some of the most moving are those born from the first-hand experience of conflict and its aftermath.

Mark Davidson's introduction to the work and to each section repays careful reading for the thoughtful insights he brings to offering prayer in times of peace and war.

*The Rt Revd Nigel Stock, Bishop at Lambeth*
*and Bishop to Her Majesty's Forces*

# *Acknowledgements*

With thanks to Mr David Blake, Curator of the Museum of Army Chaplaincy, to the staff at the Armed Forces' Chaplaincy Centre and to my father, the Revd John Davidson, for his advice on the text.

# Introduction

In August 1914, at the outset of the First World War, the Chaplain-General to the Armed Forces, John Taylor Smith, composed a six-line prayer of intercession for the soldiers of the British Expeditionary Force. 'The soldier's prayer' was printed on small cards, together with the instruction to 'slip this inside your can'. The piece Smith penned is in many ways the quintessential Christian military prayer – short, simple and robust:

> Almighty and most merciful Father,
> Forgive me my sins;
> Grant me Thy peace;
> Give me Thy power;
> Bless me in life and death,
> For Jesus Christ's sake. Amen.

Most military prayers favour function over complex imagery or profound theology. However, in spite of their simplicity, the significance of military prayers should not be underestimated. Such prayers serve two important purposes. In one respect, they fulfil a function common to all forms of prayer, namely helping

Christians to engage at a spiritual level – to articulate their concerns, to confess their failings and to ask for divine intercession. In this way, whether during peace-time or war, prayer has the capacity to enrich the life of faith by strengthening spiritual relationships and catalysing change.

However, Christian prayer within the military context also functions as a radical proclamatory act. War exists where human relationships have been torn apart. It is a weeping wound inflicted when a community or nation chooses ideology over tolerance, greed over justice, violence over negotiation. War creates a rent in human and spiritual relationships. The resultant void challenges Christian claims to divine power and love, suggesting that God is either ineffective or absent, and that humanity is beyond redemption.

But prayer serves as a radical response to such claims. Through prayer, the gospel is proclaimed into the void. This is no empty speech-act, but one which has onto-logical and incarnational consequences. By prayerful engagement with the Divine, the supplicant acknow-ledges God's ongoing authority in his or her life and invites spiritual transformation. In this sense, prayer is an act of spiritual and moral reorientation that permits personal transfiguration by the God of love. This process of transfiguration has incarnational potential; in so far as the Christian is able to embody gospel values on the battlefield, Christ is truly made present in the midst of the carnage.

*War Cries: Military prayers from barracks to battlefield* is the first volume of military prayers to be published in Britain for a wider public audience. These prayers have been gathered from more than 50 sources dating back to the 1860s. They are presented in a way that mirrors military experience, beginning with the act of 'joining up' and ending with post-conflict reflection. Although the majority of these are both British and Christian, the collection also includes a number of prayers from other nations and faith traditions. Some of the prayers are eloquent, others less so. Often, they utilize images and concepts that jar. However, regardless of their origin, style or intent, each of these prayers is valuable and is included because it offers a particular insight to prayer as it is practised within the military context.

In offering this collection, my intention is not to glorify military service, deify the dead or sanitize the horrors of war. Rather, I hope to reveal something of the realities of the Christian military life, in order to provide the Church with the language and information necessary to facilitate more meaningful dialogue with, prayer for and theological critique of the armed forces.

# 1

## *Give me, O Lord, a steadfast heart . . .*

### Prayers during training and peacetime

The military life is not an easy one and the decision to join up is never taken lightly. Throughout history, men and women have taken this step for different reasons. Some, of course, have had the choice made for them – men pressed into service in Nelson's navy, or conscripted to fight in Haig's army. Others have been driven by patriotism, by a sense of adventure, or in the hope of answering a primal *wanderlust*. Then there are those who join to better themselves, those who hope to build a career, to receive an education, or at the very least to escape from a painful past and a violent present.

Whatever their reason for joining up, those who serve in the armed forces face many challenges. The military dangers are obvious – and no less significant now than they were in bygone eras. Although British casualty rates in the Falklands, Iraq and Afghanistan have been far lower than those incurred during the world wars, the realities of death, disfigurement and disability remain no less horrendous for individuals today than they were for service personnel 100 years ago.

But these are not the only challenges associated with the military life. For some, military service poses significant physical or intellectual hurdles. In other cases, the problems are emotional or relational – with long periods away from home placing considerable strain on friendships and family ties. Often, the frustrations associated with the military lifestyle have their origins in an unavoidable clash of cultures as service personnel struggle to retain their core Christian identity and values while immersing themselves in a military idiom characterized by its own language and values, structure, traditions, lifestyle, dress code, history, laws and even humour.

The prayers listed below provide some insight to these issues. Beginning with prayers for recruits during training, they illustrate some of the emotional, moral and spiritual challenges faced by Christians serving on land, at sea and in the air.

## 1.1 For strength during training

Lord Jesus Christ, who left your home at Nazareth to fulfil your purpose, be with me now, away from those

I love. Give me your strength to go forward on my journey through life that I may fulfil the purpose you have for me. Amen.

> (The Revd Michael J. Harman RN in
> *Pray with the Navy*)

## 1.2 For those in training

O Lord, our God, we ask thy help and blessing for all who are now being prepared to take their part in the defence and service of their country. Grant that they may cheerfully perform all necessary duties; preserve them amidst the dangers and temptations which beset them; make them apt and able, that in all things they may quit themselves like men to the honour of their high calling, their country's safety, and thy glory; through him who suffered, died, and rose again for us, thy Son, our Saviour Jesus Christ. Amen.

> (*A Prayer Book for Soldiers and Sailors*, 1917)

## 1.3 For the ability to lead

Almighty God,
whose Son, the Lord of all Life,
came not to be served but to serve:
Help us to be masters of ourselves
that we may be servants of others,

and teach us to serve to lead,
through the same Jesus Christ our Lord.
Amen.

> ('The prayer of the Royal Military Academy,
> Sandhurst', from *The Armed Forces
> Simple Prayer Book*)

## 1.4 For God's blessing during training

Heavenly Father, I seek your blessing in this time of learning. Be with all on this course and those who train us. In those things which challenge us, may we know your strength; in those things we find easy, may we know your humility; in all things may we truly prepare for service to you and humankind. We make our prayer in the name of Jesus Christ. Amen.

> (The Revd Michael J. Harman RN in
> *Pray with the Navy*)

## 1.5 For airmen on their graduation

Almighty God,
you have promised that they who wait on you
shall renew their strength;
they shall rise up on wings as eagles;
they shall run and not be weary,
they shall walk and not faint.
We commend to your Fatherly protection

all who serve in the Royal Air Force
and especially today's graduating pilots and
    navigators.
Encourage and inspire us in all our efforts,
so that we may be a safeguard to our Sovereign Lady,
Queen Elizabeth,
and a sure defence to our nation.
Help us to fulfil our duties with honour,
goodwill and integrity,
and grant that we may prove worthy successors to those
who by their valour and sacrifice did nobly
save their day and generation.
Through Jesus Christ our Lord.
Amen.

('A prayer for the Royal Air Force' from
*The Armed Forces Simple Prayer Book*)

### 1.6 On going to sea

O God, I ask you to take me into your care and
    protection
along with all who sail in ships.
Make me alert and wise in my duties.
Make me faithful in times of routine
and prompt to decide
and courageous to act in any time of crisis.
Protect me in the dangers and the perils of the sea

and even in the storm grant that there may be
peace and calm within my heart.
When I am far from home and far from loved ones
and far from the country which I know,
help me to be quite sure that, wherever I am,
I can never drift beyond your care.
Take care of my loved ones in the days and weeks
    and months
when I am separated from them,
sometimes with half the world between them and me,
and every time we have to part,
bring us together in safety and in loyalty again.
This I ask for your love's sake. Amen.
    (From *Seafarers' Prayer Book* in *Pray with the Navy*)

## 1.7 For meaningful service

Lord, we know there is only one life given to each of
us. We pass by this way just once – this command,
this billet, these people – and then we move on a little
better or a little worse. We want to be able to look
back on our lives and know that our passing by has
made a difference – that we've given more than we've
taken, that we've helped more than we've hurt. Guide
us then as we try to live our lives well. Fill our days
and nights with meaning and hope as we work and
rest in your care. Amen.        (*Refuge and Strength*)

## 1.8 For those seeking promotion

Good Lord – deliver us. The promotions list comes out soon, and the days of waiting are almost over; some will receive greater rank, pay, and responsibility; some will not. We pray for all of them – that those selected will accept our praise as acknowledgement of their achievement and readiness for new responsibilities; and for those who are passed over, that they will continue to be aware of their value to us and to you, and in not losing heart, continue to strive for their chosen goals. Protect us through the night, and our loved ones, wherever they may be in your vast kingdom. And grant us peace in our time. Amen.

(*Refuge and Strength*)

## 1.9 On gaining promotion

May God, who has given me the will to undertake all these things, give me also the strength to perform them, so that he may complete the work he has begun in me through Christ our Lord. Amen.

('On promotion' from *Pray with the Navy*)

## 1.10 For the day ahead

O God, as the day returns and brings us the petty round of irritating duties, help us to perform them with laughter and kind faces; let cheerfulness abide with industry. Give us to go blithely on our business all this day, bring us to our resting beds weary and content and undishonoured, and grant us in the end the gift of sleep. We ask this in the name of Jesus Christ our Lord. Amen.

(R. L. Stevenson, 1850–94, in *Some Prayers for use in the Army Cadet Force*)

## 1.11 For divine guidance

My God, for this I pray:
Give me the light of thy love,
to shew me the path of my duty;
Give me the strength of Thy love,
to support me in the discharge of my duty;
Give me the joy of Thy love,
to help me cheerfully to accept my whole duty
to Thee, my God, and to my fellow man;
through Jesus Christ, our Lord. Amen.

(Bishop Kenneth C. Evans 'For love and duty' in *Prayers for Men in the Armed Forces*)

## 1.12 For God's gifts

O God grant to me those things,
which help me to live this day with joy and generosity.
Give me a sense of proportion,
that I may see what is important and what is not;

that I may not be irritated by things which do not
    matter.
Give me a sense of humour,
that I may learn to laugh,
and especially to laugh at myself,
and not take myself too seriously.
Give me a sense of responsibility,
that I may look on each task that comes along
as something which I am doing for the good of all
and for you.
May I not rely on our own poor resources
but on the unlimited power or your love
which you freely give me in your Holy Spirit.
I make this prayer in the name of Jesus the Lord. Amen.
    (*Armed Forces Operational Service and Prayer Book*)

## 1.13 For a dedicated heart

Give me, O Lord, a steadfast heart,
which no unworthy affection may drag downwards;
Give me an unconquered heart,
which no tribulation can wear out;
Give me an upright heart,
which no unworthy purpose may tempt aside. Amen.
                    (St Thomas Aquinas, traditional Christian
                            prayer from *Prayers for Men in
                                    the Armed Forces*)

### 1.14 For inner peace

Set free, O God, our souls from all restlessness and anxiety; that amid the storms of life we may rest in you, knowing that we are in your care, are governed by your will and guarded by your love. Amen.

(*Field Service Book*)

### 1.15 For the ability to do the right thing

Almighty and Everlasting God, by whose grace thy servants are enabled to fight the good fight of faith and ever prove victorious; we humbly beseech thee so to inspire us, that we may yield our hearts to thine obedience and exercise our wills on thy behalf. Help us to think wisely, to speak rightly, to resolve bravely, to act kindly, to live purely. Guard us in body and in soul, and make us a blessing to our fellows. Whether at home or abroad may we ever seek the extension of thy kingdom. Let the assurance of thy presence save us from sinning. O Lord our God, accept this prayer for Jesus Christ's sake. Amen.

(*Divine Service Book for the Armed Forces*)

### 1.16 For divine intervention

Lord, you are the Light of the world,
    illuminate our understanding;

10

Lord, you are the Good Shepherd,
  enfold us in your love;
Lord, you are the Way, the Truth and the Life,
  guide us along our earthly path;
Lord, you are the Bread of Life,
  fill us with your power;
Lord, you are the Resurrection and the Life,
  give us eternal life, and receive us beyond the
    gate of death. Amen.

('For guidance' from *Field Service Book*)

### 1.17  In time of temptation

O Lord, stand beside me; and when temptations come
upon me, let me feel Thy strength within me, that
I may resist all that fights against Thee and go forth
a stronger warrior because I have been tried but have
not failed. Amen.

(*Prayers for Men in the Armed Forces*)

### 1.18  For courage in everyday life

Lord, give us courage:
Courage to be gentle with people,
when it would be easier to be tough on them;
Courage to say no to what seems wrong,
when other people are eager to say yes;
Courage to do things because they are right,

even if others call us cowards for our decisions;
Courage to listen to those who are not popular or
    fashionable
when they speak unexpected wisdom;
Courage to be people of faith,
in the name of Jesus Christ. Amen.
    (*The Naval Church Service Book, Leader's Copy*)

## 1.19 For temperance

O God, who didst make man in thine own image,
and hast sanctified our human nature by the Incarnation
of thy dear Son; Give us grace to keep our bodies in
temperance and soberness. Stir up our wills to such
abstinence as may safeguard the weak. Deepen our sense
of the sinfulness of waste, and of the misery which
self indulgence thrusts upon the innocent. Strengthen
the efforts to rid our land of drunkenness; and so
mightily impel us to avoid all such things as are con-
trary to our profession, that we may prove ourselves
worthy temples of the Holy Ghost; through Jesus Christ
our Lord. Amen.
    (*A Prayer Book for Soldiers and Sailors*, 1917)

## 1.20 For guarded speech

Let me no wrong or idle word
Unthinking say,

Set Thou a seal upon my lips,
Just for to-day.
   (Chaplain Arthur Hichens in *Sunday at 09:30 Hours*)

### 1.21 For a stronger faith

Lord, I have sometimes thought,
what if you are not there at all?
Could it be true what many say,
that you do not exist at all?
I suppose it could.
And yet, at the risk of speaking into the darkness,
I ask you to give me a tiny grain of faith.
Reach out to me so that I may find you as I seek you.
I make mine the prayer of the man in the Gospel:
'Lord I believe, help my unbelief'. Amen.

('When in doubt' from *Armed Forces
Operational Service and Prayer Book*)

### 1.22 For God's purpose to be fulfilled

O Divine Creator, take into Thy holy purpose all worthy
sacrifices and heroic offerings that our men make in
defense of the weak and the oppressed, and of Thy wisdom use them for the redemption of the world in union
with the self-giving of Thy Son Christ, our Saviour. Amen.

('For Heroic Deeds' from *Prayers for
Men in the Armed Forces*)

## 1.23 The serenity prayer

God, grant me the serenity to accept the things I cannot change, the courage to change the things I can, and wisdom to know the difference. Amen.

(Reinhold Niebuhr from *Pray with the Navy*)

## 1.24 A prayer of praise and thanksgiving

Thanks be to thee, O Lord Jesus Christ,
for all the cruel pains and insults thou hast borne
    for us;
for all the many blessings thou hast won for us.
O holy Jesus,
most merciful Redeemer, friend and brother,
may we know thee more clearly,
love thee more dearly,
and follow thee more nearly, day by day. Amen.

(Prayer of Richard of Chichester from
*Refuge and Strength*)

## 1.25 For self-control

Gracious Lord, who keepest in perfect peace those whose minds are stayed on Thee, help us so to put our whole trust and confidence in Thee that we may never lose our self-possession, but that even amid the din of war our tranquil souls may hear Thy gladdening voice and be sustained by Thy life-giving word, and our faith overflow to the comfort and confidence of our comrades; through Jesus Christ, who is our peace. Amen. (*Service Hymn Book*)

## 1.26  For revival

O Lord, revive thy church, beginning with me. Amen.

('The prayer of Kagawa' from
*Refuge and Strength*)

## 1.27  For interracial harmony

Father of all men, free us from every prejudice born of hate and fear and kept alive by ignorance and pride. Open our hearts and minds to new friendships and new contributions of the spirit from men of races and cultures, religions and classes other than our own. Keep us humble to learn from the strange and unfamiliar, and never let us take cowardly refuge in half-truths and lies. Enrich us by the great thoughts and experiences of all peoples and countries. With all Thy children on the earth make us sharers of Thine abundant life and workers together in Thy Kingdom of love and peace. Amen.

('For racial cooperation' from
*Prayers for Men in the Armed Forces*)

## 1.28 A Jewish grace after meals

Blessed art thou, O Lord our God, King of the universe, who feedest the whole world with thy goodness, with grace, with lovingkindness and tender mercy; thou givest food to all flesh, for thy lovingkindness endureth for ever. Through thy great goodness food hath never failed us: O may it not fail us for ever and ever for thy great name's sake, since thou nourishest and sustainest all beings, and doest good unto all, and providest food for all thy creatures whom thou hast created. Blessed art thou, O Lord, who givest food unto all.

*(Prayer Book for Jewish Sailors and Soldiers)*

## 1.29 A military grace

Bless this food and bless this wine;
Bless us with your love divine.
Keep us righteous, chaste and sober . . .
. . . at least until this meal is over.
Amen.

(Contemporary naval grace, used at
Royal Marine Condor, 2015)

## 1.30 For relations and friends

O Lord our God who art in every place and from whom no space or distance can ever separate us; we know that they who are absent from each other are still present with thee. Protect and bless our friends and relations from whom we are separated at this time; keep them both in body and soul and grant that both they and we, by drawing near to thee, may draw near to each other, knit together by the unseen chain of thy love, the communion of thy saints and the holy Fellowship of thy Spirit: grant, if it be thy will, that we may meet again on earth and finally live together in thy heavenly kingdom; through Jesus Christ our Lord. Amen.

(Sir William Martin, Chief Justice
of New Zealand, 1879, in
*The Army Prayer Book, India*)

## 1.31 For home and loved ones

O Heavenly Father who hast bestowed upon us the blessing of relations and friends, look we beseech thee with eyes of compassion on our loved ones from whom we are now separated. Be pleased, we pray thee, to pour down upon them the abundance of thy mercy – abide with them and bless them and let thy heavenly peace rest in their hearts. By thy good Spirit, enable us to keep faith with them, in purity, honour and truth, and mercifully grant, if it be thy will, that when we have done our duty, we may be restored to them again. Through Jesus Christ our Lord. Amen.

(*Divine Service Book for the Armed Forces*)

### 1.32 For absent friends

O Lord God Almighty, who dwellest in love and abidest in peace, whose gift it is that the bond of affection is not severed by bodily absence, and the flame of sacred love is not extinguished by parting, but rather increased by longing remembrance; We pray thee that unwearied affection may remain in us true and pure, ever calling the absent to loving remembrance and keeping present in our hearts those who art far away; Be pleased, O Lord, to prosper the course of our loved ones, thy servants, and to keep and defend them from all snares of the enemy; through Jesus Christ our Lord. Amen.

('For friends' from *The Army Prayer Book, India*)

### 1.33 For mothers

Lord Jesus, Thou hast known
A mother's love and tender care,
And Thou wilt hear while for my own mother
    most dear
I make this Sabbath prayer.
Protect her life, I pray,

Who gave the gift of life to me;
And may she know from day to day the deepening
  glow
Of joy that comes from Thee.
I cannot pay my debt
For all the love that she has given;
But Thou, love's Lord, wilt not forget her due reward –
Bless her in earth and heaven. Amen.

  (Henry Van Dyke in *The Hymnal Army and Navy*)

### 1.34 For family life

O Father of all, make me a good parent to my children. Give my *husband/wife* all the help *he/she* needs when I am at sea or away from home. Let my times at home be times of happiness and opportunities for the renewal of love between each of us, my *husband/wife* and our children. As long as I go out to sea may it be my constant joy to return home to those whom you have given me as my own, through Jesus Christ our Lord. Amen.                    (*Pray with the Navy*)

### 1.35 For those at home

Almighty God, Father of our Lord Jesus Christ, of whom the whole family in earth and heaven is named; We commend to thee our loved ones at home. Guard and protect them from all evil. Amid all the separations of this life, keep them and us under thy care and guidance; watch over them and us while we are absent one from the other. Grant us a happy reunion here on earth, and after the separation of this life, unite us all at last in thy heavenly kingdom; through Jesus Christ our Lord. Amen.

(*A Prayer Book for Soldiers and Sailors*, 1917)

### 1.36 For families

Lord, it's hard to think of those at home without feeling alone. Help me to remember them with thankfulness, knowing that in their hearts and mine, the distance between us is really very short. Thank you for those whom I miss; thank you for the value they give to my life; thank you for the good memories of times spent with them; thank you that I may look forward to time spent with them in the future. Help me to remember that with you beside me, and them thinking of me, I am never alone. Amen.

(The Revd Alison E. P. Norman RN in
*Pray with the Navy*)

### 1.37 Prayer before sleep

Dear God, as I lay me down to sleep,
relax the tension of my body;
calm the restlessness of my mind;

still the thoughts which worry and perplex me.
Help me to rest myself and all my problems in your
strong and loving arms.
Let your Spirit speak to my mind and heart while
    I am asleep,
so that, when I wake up in the morning,
I may find that I have received in the night-time,
light for my way;
strength for my tasks;
peace for my worries;
forgiveness for my sins.
Grant me sleep tonight, and tomorrow power to live.
Amen.                    (ChaplainCare website)

### 1.38 An evening prayer

Lord, it is late and I am tired and far from home.
I am lonely and among strangers.
The day that is past was the usual mixture;
I am not proud of everything I did or said.
I have not always been aware of myself,
of why I did the things I did or adopted certain
    attitudes.
Stay with me to calm me down,
and see me safely asleep.
Bless me with a restful night.
Awaken me to a new day with a glad heart,

putting behind me my yesterday,
and resolved to live the next at peace with you
and all your creation.
For I know your Holy Spirit is with me
and his power is sufficient for all good things
if I but let him work in me. Amen.

(*Armed Forces Operational Service and Prayer Book*)

## 1.39 A prayer at Taps

Before we go to rest we commit ourselves to thy care,
O God our Father, beseeching Thee through Jesus
Christ our Lord to keep alive thy grace in our hearts.
Watch Thou, O Heavenly Father, with those who
wake, or watch, or weep to-night, and give thine angels
charge over those who sleep. Tend those who are sick,
rest those who are weary, soothe those who suffer,
pity those in affliction; be near and bless those who
are dying, and keep under thy holy care those who are
dear to us. Through Christ our Lord. Amen.

('Prayer at Taps' from *The Hymnal Army and Navy*)

## 1.40 When unable to sleep

Father, I am restless and unable to sleep.
So much is going through my mind.
But I know that you are here with me,
that you never leave my side.

22

Calm my mind.
Take away the worry and restlessness.
Grant me some restful sleep,
even for just a few hours.
When I rise,
remind me of how close you are to me.
Into your hands I commend my spirit. Amen.
 (*Armed Forces Operational Service and Prayer Book*)

# 2

## *Preserve us . . . from the violence of the enemy . . .*

### Prayers for the quarterdeck and airfield

The plethora of chapels and churches in Britain's coastal towns testifies to the strength of faith within our nation's seafaring communities. This is true of both our merchant fleet and Royal Navy. Within the latter, religious observance was for many years protected by the Articles of War of 1653, the first of which declares that the Lord's Day shall be observed on all naval vessels. Although historically important, from a spiritual perspective, this law merely reflected the normative nature of faith at sea. In British waters, this history can be traced back a further thousand years, with Bede referring to ministry at sea as early as 651. Arguably, the illustrious history of naval chaplaincy can be traced back to biblical times, with Jesus' work among the Galilean fishermen (Luke 5.1–11) and St Paul's ministry to sailors (Acts 27.27–44).

The spiritual aspect of naval life is reflected in many of the prayers included in this section. It begins with the most famous of them all, the Naval Prayer of 1662. Although this prayer has been modified over the years to reflect changes in sovereignty and geography, the core values expressed within it remain as true for contemporary sailors, submariners and marines as they were for the Royal Navy 350 years ago – loyalty to the crown, respect for the elements and a commitment to protect all civilian traffic upon the high seas.

This section also includes several prayers for airmen and the Royal Air Force. Although the RAF lacks the history and tradition of prayer associated with the Royal Navy, the prayers that they have produced remind us that those serving in the Air Force face similar challenges to their compatriots serving at sea. Whether flying combat operations, or fulfilling the more mundane task of moving troops and equipment around the world, those who serve in the air are well aware of the fragility of both crew and craft, the dangers posed by capricious weather systems, and the unforgiving nature of warfare when conducted away from dry land.

## 2.1 The Naval Prayer

O Eternal Lord God, who alone spreadest out the heavens, and rulest the raging of the Sea; who hast compassed the waters with bounds until day and night come to an end; be pleased to receive into thy Almighty and most gracious protection the persons of us thy servants and the Fleet in which we serve. Preserve us from the dangers of the sea and of the air and from the violence of the enemy; that we may be a safeguard unto our most gracious Sovereign Lady, Queen Elizabeth, and her Dominions, and a security for such as pass on the seas upon their lawful occasions; that the inhabitants of our islands and Commonwealth may in peace and quietness serve thee, our God; and that we may return in safety to enjoy the blessings of the land, with the fruits of our labours and with a thankful remembrance of thy mercies to praise and glorify thy holy name; through Jesus Christ our Lord. Amen.

(Contemporary version of the Naval Prayer, originally from the 1662 Book of Common Prayer, in *The Naval Church Service Book, Leader's Copy*)

## 2.2 The Royal Marines' Prayer

O Eternal Lord God, who through many generations hast united and inspired the Members of our Corps, grant Thy Blessing we beseech Thee on Royal Marines serving all around the Globe. Bestow Thy crown of

Righteousness upon all our efforts and endeavours, and may our Laurels be those of gallantry and honour, loyalty and courage. We ask these in the name of Him, whose courage never failed, our Redeemer, Jesus Christ. Amen.

(Traditional prayer of the Royal Marines from *Commando Prayer Book*)

## 2.3 For submariners

O Father, hear our prayer to Thee
From your humble servants beneath the sea.
In the depths of ocean oft we stray,
So far from night, so far from day;
We would ask your guiding light to glow,
To make our journey safe below.
Please oft times grant us patient mind,
Then 'ere the darkness, won't us blind.
We seek thy protection from the deep
And grant us peace whene'er we sleep.
Of our homes and loved ones far away,
We ask you care for them each day,
Until we surface once again,
To drink the air and feel the rain.
We ask your guiding hand to show
A safe progression, sure and slow.
Dear Lord, please hear our prayer to Thee

From your humble servants beneath the sea.

Amen.

> (Traditional prayer of the Submarine
> Service, Royal Navy)

## 2.4  The Royal Air Force, Collect 1

Almighty God, who has promised that they who wait upon thee shall renew their strength and mount up with wings, as eagles, we commend to thy fatherly protection all who serve in the Royal Air Force. Uplift and support us in our endeavour, that we may be a safeguard unto our most gracious Sovereign Lady Queen Elizabeth and a sure defence to our homeland. Help us to fulfil our several duties with honour, goodwill and integrity, and grant that we may prove to be worthy successors of those who by their valour and sacrifice did nobly save their day and generation; through Jesus Christ our Lord. Amen.    (RAF Chaplaincy website)

## 2.5  For the airmen and others in hazardous service

O Almighty God, who sittest on thy throne judging right; We commend to thy fatherly goodness the men serving our Nation at this time of peril (particularly our Airmen and others in hazardous employ) beseeching thee to take into thine own hand both them and the cause which they uphold. Be thou their tower of strength and give them courage in peril and danger. Make them bold through life or death to put their trust in thee, who art the giver of all victory; through Jesus Christ our Lord. Amen.

(*A Prayer Book for Soldiers and Sailors*, 1917)

## 2.6 For our ship

Almighty Father, look, we pray you, upon this ship and grant that all who live and serve in her may be true to the example your Son has set for us. Take from us all selfishness and jealousy which may prevent unity and fellowship. This we ask for Jesus' sake. Amen.

('Our ship' from *Pray with the Navy*)

## 2.7 During a storm

O most powerful and glorious Lord God, at whose command the winds blow and lift up the waves of the sea, and who stillest the rage thereof; we, thy creatures, but miserable sinners, do in this our great distress cry unto thee for help: Save, Lord, or else we perish. We confess when we have been safe, and seen all things quiet about us, we have forgotten thee, our God, and refused to hearken to the still voice of thy Word, and to obey thy commandments; but now we see how terrible thou art in all thy works of wonder; the great God to be feared above all; and therefore we adore thy

Divine Majesty, acknowledging thy power, and imploring thy goodness. Help, Lord, and save us for thy
mercies' sake, in Jesus Christ, thy Son our Lord. Amen.
(*The Soldier's Prayer Book*)

## 2.8 For deliverance from a storm

Thou, O Lord, who stillest the raging of the sea,
hear, hear us, and save us, that we perish not.
O blessed Savior,
who didst save Thy disciples ready to perish in a storm,
hear us, and save us we beseech Thee.
Lord, have mercy upon us.
Christ, have mercy upon us.
Lord, have mercy upon us.
O Lord, hear us.
O Christ, hear us.
God the Father, God the Son, God the Holy Ghost,
have mercy upon us,
save us now and evermore.
Amen.

('Short prayers amidst a storm' from
*Service Prayer Book*)

## 2.9 A Royal Air Force prayer of rededication

Lord God, we remember the courage and dedication of
those who in past days took to the air, and pioneered

the Royal Air Force we know today. Especially we remember the sacrifice of the few for the many in times of war and strife. Grant that, being inspired by their example, we may follow them in their endeavours to work for a world in which peace and justice reign supreme, through Jesus Christ our Lord. Amen.

('Prayer for the foundation of the Royal Air Force' from *The Armed Forces Simple Prayer Book*)

## 2.10 Marine prayer

Almighty Father, whose command is over all and whose love never fails, make me aware of Thy presence and obedient to Thy will. Keep me true to my best self, guarding me against dishonesty in purpose and deed and helping me to live so that I can face my fellow Marines, my loved ones and Thee without shame or fear. Protect my family. Give me the will to do the work of a Marine and to accept my share of responsibilities with vigor and enthusiasm. Grant me the courage to be proficient in my daily performance. Keep me loyal and faithful to my superiors and to the duties my country and the Marine Corps have entrusted to me. Make me considerate of those committed to my leadership. Help me to wear my uniform with dignity, and let it remind me daily of the traditions which I must uphold. If I am inclined to doubt, steady my faith; if I am tempted, make me strong to resist; if I should miss the mark, give me courage to try again. Guide me with the light of truth and grant me wisdom by which I may understand the answer to my prayer. Amen.

('Marine prayer', ChaplainCare website)

## 2.11 The Royal Air Force Regiment's Collect

Almighty God, Lord of heaven and earth, whose son Jesus Christ showed us the path of duty, we beseech thee to bless all who serve in the Royal Air Force Regiment. Help us to do our duty with courage and dedication. Of thy goodness be our strength in times of danger, watch over our loved ones when we are separated, and make us a sure defence to those we serve. We ask this in the name of Jesus Christ our Lord. Amen.

(Contemporary RAF Collect from
*The Armed Forces Simple Prayer Book*)

## 2.12 For those at sea during conflict

O Thou that slumberest not nor sleepest, protect, we pray thee, our sailors from the sudden perils of the sea, from the snares and assaults of the enemy. In the anxious hours of waiting, steady and support those on whom the burdens of responsibility lie heavily; and grant that in dangers often, in watchings often, in weariness often, they may serve thee with a quiet mind; through Jesus Christ our Lord. Amen.

*(Army Prayer Book)*

## 2.13 For airmen

Almighty God, who makest the clouds thy chariot and walkest upon the wings of the wind; have mercy, we beseech thee, on our airmen, and when they are amidst the clouds and wonders of the sky, give unto them the assurance of thy protection, that they may do their duty with prudence and with fearlessness, confident that in life or in death the eternal God is their refuge, and underneath are the everlasting arms; through Jesus Christ our Lord. Amen.

('For the Air Force' from *Divine Service Book for the Armed Forces*)

## 2.14 The Naval Collect

Go before us, O Lord, in all our doings, with Thy most gracious favours and further us with Thy continual help that in all our works begun, continued and ended in Thee, we may glorify Thy holy name and finally, by Thy mercy, obtain everlasting life; through Jesus Christ our Lord. Amen. (Traditional Collect)

## 2.15 The Commando Prayer

Almighty God, whose command is overall and whose love never fails, let me not pray to be sheltered from dangers but to be fearless in facing them. Let me not beg for the stilling of pain but for the heart to conquer it. Let me not avoid my share of responsibilities but embrace them with a strong heart and cheerful mind. Let me not always seek my own ends but help me to be considerate of the needs of others. Let me not fail those who have placed their trust in me but let my Green Beret remind me daily of the high traditions of Commando service. And if I fail, give me the courage and the faith to try again. Guide me with the light of your truth and keep before me the example of Jesus Christ in whose name I pray. Amen.

(*Commando Prayer Book*)

## 2.16 The prayer of a Bluejacket

Our Father, which art in heaven, I bow reverently to ask that Thou wilt give me Thy blessing and Thy benediction. Forgive, I pray, my sins; those of which I am aware and those of which I may have no consciousness of guilt. I thank Thee for the privilege which is mine of wearing this uniform and of serving in our Navy. I am proud of the fact that I was found capable and worthy of being counted among those who help to preserve and carry on the high and noble traditions of the naval service.

Bless our Command and our comrades of the service, wherever they may be today, ashore and at sea. Help me at all times in my dealings with my shipmates and with others to be honourable, considerate and fair. Inspire me so that I may keep my mind clean and my heart pure, and thus be enabled to walk uprightly from day to day.

Keep me strong, fearless and faithful ever to my Country and to Thee. And, dear Heavenly Father, I pray especially that Thou wilt watch over, protect, and guard, during my absence from home, those whom I love. In Jesus' name I pray. Amen.

(*Song and Service Book for Ship and Field*)

## 2.17 For the Royal Air Force

O God who spreadest out the heavens like a curtain, and makest man to be an inheritor of the trackless air, as of the land and the deep sea; sustain in Thy gracious keeping the men of the Royal Air Force. Match their courage and skill with Thy spirit of merciful love; in danger protect them and in responsibility inspire them. Make them to know that in the skies as on dry land they are sustained by the arms of Thy everlasting love; through Jesus Christ our Lord. Amen.

('For airmen' from *The Scottish Service Book*)

## 2.18 For the Royal Naval Reserve

Almighty God who wills that all should dwell in safety, we hold in prayer before you all members of the Royal Naval Reserve; remembering them wherever they are throughout the world and the Divisions in which they serve. Grant that through their fellowship of service to our Commonwealth they may find true friends; and being trained to take their part in our defence by sea, may prove themselves enduring, skilled and resolute in war and peace; through him who came to serve and give his life as a ransom for many, Jesus Christ our Lord. Amen. (*Pray with the Navy*)

## 2.19 Nelson's grace

God save the Queen.
Bless our victuals,
God protect the Fleet in which we serve.
Amen.

(Historic naval grace from *The Naval Officer's Little Book of Graces*)

## 2.20 The Royal Air Force, Collect 2

Almighty God, who makest the clouds thy chariots and walkest upon the wings of the storm, look in mercy we beseech thee upon the Royal Air Force. Make us a tower of strength to our Queen and to our country.

Help us to do our duty with prudence and with fearlessness, confident that in life or in death the eternal God is our refuge and strength. Grant this for Jesus Christ's sake. Amen.

(Contemporary RAF Collect from
*The Armed Forces Simple Prayer Book*)

## 2.21 An ecumenical Eucharistic Prayer

We come together drawn from many Christian traditions and none. We come to share the bread and the wine as Jesus asked us to do. For some, this bread and wine are powerful symbols of God's love for them and all humanity. For others, the bread and wine truly become the body and blood of Christ, our spiritual nourishment. For still others it is both. Lord, we ask that you send your Spirit upon these gifts and upon ourselves, that they may be your symbol of love to us, your spiritual food for us, and that we may know your presence with us, uniting us in Christ. Amen.

(Prayer used on Easter Sunday by chaplains
of 3 Commando Brigade, Iraq, 2003,
from *Commando Prayer Book*)

## 2.22 For a safe return from sea

O Eternal Father, who shewest thy wondrous power and mercy to those who go down to the sea in ships:

We give thee humble thanks for that thou hast been pleased to preserve through the perils of the deep these thy servants who now desire to offer their praises and thanksgivings unto thee. Grant that they may be ever mindful of thy merciful providence towards them, and express their thankfulness by a living trust in thee, and obedience to thy laws; through Jesus Christ our Lord. Amen.

*(Divine Service Book for the Armed Forces)*

## 2.23 For the Merchant Navy

Remember, O Lord, our loved ones in distant lands. Sweeten, we beseech Thee, the bitterness of long separation; watch over children far from fathers and mothers; help and protect parted parents. Speed the months and years that may lie between sad partings and joyful reunions; strengthen the ties that bind families together though loved ones be far asunder. May duty to Thee guide those that are lonely; and grant that neither we nor those we love may falter in our devotion to each other or to Thee. We pray that the weariness of separation may never weaken our sense of duty, and we beseech Thee to sustain us always by the sure knowledge that underneath are the everlasting arms; through Jesus Christ our Lord. Amen.

*(The Scottish Service Book)*

## 2.24 For the Special Boat Service

We do not seek an easy life. Rather we pray for courage to face every task as and when it may arise. Bless our loved ones and may they know how much we appreciate them. Equip us to resist evil, protect the vulnerable, pursue what is right, with guile to use our strength wisely. And guard us with humility, that we may not think of ourselves more highly than we ought, nor underestimate others. So enrich our knowledge of you our Creator that we may acknowledge the Holy Spirit as friend and guide, for the sake of Christ our Saviour. Amen.

('An SBS prayer' from *Pray with the Navy*)

## 2.25 The Royal Air Force, Collect 3

Holy Spirit, Breath of God, who dost inspire and sustain man's destiny; quicken, we beseech Thee, the hearts and minds of all who serve in the Royal Air Force; that those who fly may brave the perils of the air with courage; that those who labour on the ground may be infused with zeal and devotion; and that all who bear the burden and heat of the day may be refreshed with the life-giving power of thy grace; through Jesus Christ our Lord. Amen.

(Contemporary RAF Collect from
*The Armed Forces Simple Prayer Book*)

## 2.26 For the Fleet Air Arm

O God, who dwells above the water and has the power to still the raging of the sea, accept the prayers of all your servants who commit their lives to the dangers of the sea and air. In all their ways, enable them to serve you in a godly and faithful way, and in their Christian lives reflect your glory throughout the world. Through all their journeys, watch over them that they may overcome evil, temptation or anything that harms their souls, so that through all the changes and chances of this life, you will bring them by your mercy to the sure promise of your everlasting kingdom, through Jesus Christ our Lord. Amen.

('The Fleet Air Arm' from *Pray with the Navy*)

## 2.27 For the Coastguard service

Almighty and Everlasting God, Whose hand stills the tumult of the deep, we offer our prayers for those who serve in our Coast Guard. We are mindful of their traditions of selfless service to the seafarers who make their ways to appointed ports. Employ their devotions of good ends as they track the weather and search the seas for those in extremity of storm, shipwreck or battle. Make their soundings and markings sure that safe passages may be found by those who go down to the sea in ships. Encourage them, O Lord, as they stand guard over our coasts and the bulwarks of our freedoms. Graciously deliver them from the threatening calamities in all their perilous voyages. Bless the keepers of the lights and be Thou their close friend in lonely watches. Keep the beacons of honor and duty burning that they may reach the home port with duty well performed, in service to Thee and our land.

('A USCG prayer', ChaplainCare website)

### 2.28 A Trafalgar Night grace

As Nelson's vict'ry we recall
We ask Thy blessing, Lord of all,
That all who in this meal do share
Might e'er enjoy Thy tender care.
Thus evermore shall rise to Thee,
Glad hymns of praise from land and sea.
Amen.

(Traditional naval grace from *The Naval Officer's Little Book of Graces*)

### 2.29 For other seafarers

We pray, O God, for all seafarers as they fulfil the duties and face the dangers of their calling: the officers and men of the Merchant Navy; the Royal Fleet Auxiliary; the keepers of lighthouses and crews of lightships and weatherships; the pilots of our ports; all who carry out the services of docks and harbours; and those who man lifeboats and guard our coasts. Grant them your strength and protection and keep them in the hours of special need; for Jesus Christ's sake. Amen.

*(Pray with the Navy)*

## 2.30 A marine's prayer

Dear God, in a world that's racked with war,
Let me think of the coming years
When the cannon's core has ceased its roar,
And the nations dry their tears.
Keep Thou my heart unblemished.
Give me strength to wait release;
And let me live as a man should live
In a fight for the God of Peace.
O Father, grant that I may last
To build the world again;
To know when pestilence is past
A brotherhood of men.
Bless Thou the aged with Thy light;
Protect our troubled youth;
And let me fight as a man should fight
In a war for the God of Truth.
Thy will be done, if Thou decree
That I shall die afield.

But let me go face to the foe
Sustain me, lest I yield.
Let no man cry he saw me fly
The battle's agony.
And let me die as a man should die
In a fight for Liberty. Amen.

('Marine's prayer II', ChaplainCare website)

## 2.31 A submariner's prayer

Lord, thou commanded us saying 'thou shalt not kill'. Thou knowest that we prepare ourselves constantly to kill, not one but thousands, and that by this preparation we believe that we help to preserve peace among nations. Do thou, who gave man the knowledge to fashion this terrible weapon, give him also the sense of responsibility to control its use; so that fear of the consequences may indeed maintain peace until that day when love, not fear, shall control all men's actions. Give us the will, but never the wish, to obey the order to fire. Oh God, if it is thy will, grant that that order may never need to be given.

(Captain M. C. Henry RN, the first commanding officer of *HMS Resolution*, prayer now displayed in the chapel of *HMS Neptune*)

# 3

*You strode before us down that dreadful road . . .*

## Army and Tri-Service prayers

The prayers in this section fall into two distinct categories – general prayers used by soldiers or military personnel involved in land operations, and prayers particular to specific regiments. The more general prayers cover a broad range of scenarios including prayers for personnel in camp, for those in transit and for all those serving oversees. The section ends with a poignant personal prayer written by an unknown author, grateful to have survived Dunkirk, but facing an uncertain future.

Many of the regimental Collects included here are the work of one man, the Revd Matthew Tobias. In each case he drew inspiration from the regiment's cap badge. These badges include symbols illustrating a unit's origins, values, motto or greatest exploits. In this way, Tobias created contextual prayers which got to the very heart of the regiment's identity, and so resonated strongly with those who used them. Although originally published in 1930, Tobias's work remains apropos today, and in many cases the current regimental Collects remain virtually unchanged, with only slight alterations in language or style. In other cases, where units have been amalgamated, an attempt has been made to preserve key elements from both of the original Collects.

## 3.1 A soldier's morning prayer

Shorter Form of Morning Prayer For Those Who Are Much Pressed For Time. *If time does not allow of longer Devotions, the Christian Soldier will, when dressed, kneel down, placing himself in thought in the Presence of God . . . and say:*

Lord, have mercy upon me.
Christ, have mercy upon me.
Lord, have mercy upon me.

O Lord, turn Thy face from my sins;
And put out all my misdeeds.
O God, make clean my heart within me;
And take not Thy Holy Spirit from me.
Lord, hear my prayer;
And let my cry come unto Thee.

Prayer. Most gracious God and Merciful Father, I give Thee thanks for Thy protection during the night past, and for all Thy countless Mercies. Defend me, this day, from every danger, and keep me from offending Thee in word or deed. Hold Thou up my goings in Thy paths. Teach me to do Thy will cheerfully in all things: and let Thy blessing be upon me, and all that belong to me, this day and for evermore. Amen.

Be Thou, O Lord,
Within me, to strengthen me;
Without me, to keep me;
Above me, to protect me;
Beneath me, to uphold me;
Before me, to lead me;
Behind me, to keep me;
Round about me, to defend me.

Our Father . . .

> (The Rev. C. Walford MA, Chaplain Bombay,
> *The Christian Soldier's Manual of Prayer*)

## 3.2 A Collect for the armed forces

Almighty God, protect all who serve in Her Majesty's Forces; strengthen us in danger and temptation; give us courage and loyalty, that we may remain true to the highest traditions of our profession; and keep us steadfast when faced with the perils of action in war; through Jesus Christ our Lord. Amen.

> (Collect from 'A Service for use on operations' from *Armed Forces Operational Service and Prayer Book*)

### 3.3 Collect of the Life Guards

O Ever-living God, King of kings, in whose service we put on the breastplate of faith and love, and for a helmet the hope of salvation, grant we beseech thee that The Life Guards may be faithful unto death, and at last receive the crown of life from Jesus Christ, our Lord.

> (Contemporary version of the regimental Collect)

### 3.4 Collect of the Royal Scots Greys (2nd Dragoons)

Almighty God, King of kings and Lord of lords, give thy grace, we pray thee, to the Royal Scots Greys, that we may be second to none in obedience to thy will, but swifter than eagles to overtake thine enemies and spoil the powers of evil, in the strength of Jesus Christ our Lord.

> (Historical version of the regimental Collect from *Collects for the British Army*)

### 3.5 For soldiers

O God, who seest that in this warfare we are seeking to serve Thee, and yet in the waging of it must needs do many things that are an offence against Thy love; accept we pray Thee, our imperfect offering. Arm us with Thy spirit that our warfare may further the victory of Thy justice and truth; through Jesus Christ our Lord. Amen.

(*The Pocket Padre*)

### 3.6 Collect of the Grenadier Guards

O God, the father of our Lord Jesus Christ, who has taught us that the stronger may come upon the strong and take from him all his armour wherein he trusted, grant that thy servants, the Grenadier Guards, may ever trust in thy everlasting strength to overcome the enemy of our souls, through the same Jesus Christ our redeemer.

(Historical form of the regimental Collect from *Collects for the British Army*)

### 3.7 Collect of the Royal Irish Regiment

Almighty God, whose love knows no bounds, grant that we, the Royal Irish Regiment, may do our duty courageously whether at home or abroad, so that undaunted by the difficulties which beset us, your will may be done. And united as members one with another, may we, mindful of the valour and sacrifice of those who have gone before us, clear the way for those that follow; through Jesus Christ, our Lord. Amen.

(Contemporary version of the regimental Collect)

## 3.8 Collect of the Black Watch (Royal Highlanders)

O God, whose strength setteth fast the mountains, give thy grace, we pray thee, to the Black Watch, once chosen to guard the mountains for our King, that we may stand fast in the faith and be strong, as we watch for the coming of him who has bidden us watch and pray, our saviour Jesus Christ.

(Historical form of the regimental Collect
from *Collects for the British Army*)

## 3.9 For the forces of the king

O Lord God, high and mighty, who doest thy will in the army of heaven and amongst the inhabitants of the earth; stretch forth the shield of thy protection over those who serve the King in defending our shores and guarding our homes. Lead and guide them by thy counsel; strengthen and defend them with thy might; that they may steadfastly continue an honour and protection to the people; and that under thy governance they may be called to no service but the just and peaceable maintenance of order; through Jesus Christ our Lord. Amen.

*(Divine Service Book for the Armed Forces)*

## 3.10 Collect of the Military Provost Staff Corps

Almighty God, whose ways are justice and peace and whose judgments are righteous and merciful, grant to us thy servants of the Military Provost Staff Corps, the spirit of understanding and compassion, that by thy inspiration we may be faithful in the discharge of our duties, zealous in protection of the weak and faint-hearted, and selfless in serving the best interests of those who have brought judgment upon themselves. We ask this in the Name, and in the service, of our Lord and Saviour, Jesus Christ. Amen.

(Historical version of the Collect for Military Police)

## 3.11 A soldier's prayer for divine inspiration

Almighty and everlasting God, by whose grace thy servants are enabled to fight the good fight of faith and ever prove victorious: We humbly beseech thee so to inspire us, that we may yield our hearts to thine obedience and exercise our wills on thy behalf. Help us to think wisely: to speak rightly: to resolve bravely: to act kindly: to live purely. Bless us in body and in soul, and make us a blessing to our comrades. Whether at home or abroad may we ever seek the extension of thy kingdom. Let the assurance of thy presence save us from sinning: strengthen us in life, and comfort us in death. O Lord our God, accept this prayer for Jesus Christ's sake. Amen.

(*A Form of Prayer for Open Air Services*, 1915)

## 3.12 Collect of the Welsh Guards

O Lord God, who hast given us the land of our fathers for our inheritance, help thy servants, the Welsh Guards, to keep thy laws as our heritage for ever, until we come to that better and heavenly country which thou has prepared for us; through Jesus Christ our Lord.

(*Collects for the British Army*)

## 3.13 Collect of the Scots Guards

Almighty God, whose blessed son did say unto Saint Andrew 'follow me,' grant that the Scots Guards who wear the cross of thy Holy Apostle may follow thy son with impunity, be made stronger in brotherhood and fierce against all enemies of our Saviour; ever going forward under his leadership who by the hard and painful way of the cross won high conquest and great glory, even Jesus Christ our Lord.

(An alternative form of the regimental Collect, by D. H. Whiteford, handwritten in *Collects for the British Army*)

## 3.14 A soldier's prayer for good conduct

Almighty God,

Whose command is overall and whose love never fails,

Let me be aware of your presence and obedient to
  your will.

Help me to accept my share of responsibility

With strong heart and cheerful mind.

Make me considerate of those with whom I live and
  serve,

And faithful to the duties my country has entrusted
  to me.

Let my uniform remind me daily

of the traditions of the Army in which I serve.

When I am tempted to sin, let me resist.

When I fail, give me courage to try again.

Guide me with the light of your truth,

And keep before me the example of Jesus

In whose name I pray and in whom I trust.

('Soldier's Prayer' in *The Armed Forces
Simple Prayer Book*)

## 3.15 Collect of the Royal Armoured Corps

Almighty God, who art our defence and our castle,
grant to the Royal Armoured Corps that putting on
the whole armour of God they may go forth through

the earth eager to do thee service with courage and faith, and never be separated from thy grace or divided among themselves, through Jesus Christ Our Lord to whom, with the Father and Holy Spirit one blessed and eternal Trinity, be glory for ever. Amen.

(Contemporary version of the Corps' Collect)

## 3.16 Collect of the Army Catering Corps

O God, creator and sustainer of all life, grant unto us of the Army Catering Corps, grace to set duty above selfish desires and steadfastness of purpose above weariness; that faithfully fulfilling the tasks entrusted to us, we may minister to the needs of others for the honour of our Corps and the glory of thy Holy name, through Jesus Christ our Lord. Amen. (Historical Collect of the Corps)

## 3.17 For the Army

O Lord God of Hosts, stretch forth, we pray thee, thine almighty arm, to strengthen and protect the soldiers of our King in every peril; shelter them in the day of battle, and in time of peace keep them safe from all evil; endue them ever with loyalty and courage, and grant that in all things they may serve as seeing thee; through Jesus Christ our Lord. Amen.

(*Divine Service Book for the Armed Forces*)

## 3.18 Collect of the Army Chaplains' Department

Blessed God, who has committed the glorious Gospel to our trust, have mercy upon the Royal Army Chaplains' Department and grant that we may never glory save in the Cross of our Lord Jesus Christ, but in all things may approve ourselves as thy ministers, through the same thy Son Jesus Christ our Lord. Amen.

(Contemporary version of the Chaplains' Collect)

## 3.19 Collect of the Royal Army Medical Corps

O God, whose blessed son was made perfect through suffering, give thy grace, we beseech thee, to thy servants of the Royal Army Medical Corps, that, by loyalty in hard service after the example of Saint Luke the beloved physician, we may be found faithful in ministering to those that need, for his sake who went about doing good, the same thy son Jesus Christ our Lord.

(*Collects for the British Army*)

## 3.20 Collect of the Special Air Service Regiment

O Lord who didst call on thy disciples to venture all to win all men to thee, grant that we, the chosen members of the Special Air Service Regiment, may by our works and ways dare all to win all, and in doing so render special service to thee and our fellow-men in all the world, through the same Jesus Christ our Lord. Amen.

(Contemporary version of the regimental Collect)

### 3.21 For military chaplains

Almighty and everlasting God, who by thy Holy Spirit didst preside over the first gathering of the Apostles at Jerusalem, and hast promised to be with thy Church always even unto the end of the world: vouchsafe, we beseech thee, to be with us who are Chaplains to the Armed Forces of our Country. Grant unto us thy gracious presence and blessing. Deliver us from all error, pride and prejudice; enlighten us with thy wisdom, and so order all our doing that thy kingdom may be advanced.

Make us considerate of those whom thou hast entrusted to us, and faithful to the duties laid upon us by our country. Let our uniform remind us daily of the traditions of our Service. Grant us thy Grace that we may lead many to thee, and that we may touch many lives by the life we lead, the deeds we do and the words we say.

Guide us with the light of truth and keep before us the life of him by whose example and help we trust to obtain the answer to our prayers, Jesus Christ our Lord. Amen.

('The chaplains' prayer' from *Divine Service Book for The Armed Forces*)

### 3.22 Collect of the Royal Army Pay Corps

Lord Jesus Christ, prince of the kings of the earth, who hast bidden us render to Caesar the things that are Caesar's, assist with thy grace thy servants of the Royal Army Pay Corps, that, rendering to God the things that are God's, we may render to all their dues, as faithful and wise stewards to whom thou wilt entrust the true riches, who with the Father and the Holy Ghost livest and reignest for ever.

(Historical collect from *Collects for the British Army*)

### 3.23 For sailors, soldiers and airmen

O Lord God of Hosts, stretch forth, we pray thee, thine Almighty arm to strengthen and protect the sailors, and soldiers of our King in every peril of land, and sea, and air; shelter them in the day of battle, and in time of peace keep them safe from all evil; endue them ever with loyalty and courage, and grant that in all things they may serve as seeing thee, who art invisible; through Jesus Christ our Lord. Amen.

(From *Prayer Book of Church of Scotland*, 1912,
in *The Army Prayer Book, India*)

## 3.24 For the US Armed Forces

Almighty God, we commend to your gracious care and keeping all the men and women of our armed forces at home and abroad. Defend them day by day with your heavenly grace; strengthen them in their trials and temptations; give them courage to face the perils which beset them; and grant them a sense of your abiding presence wherever they may be; through Jesus Christ our Lord. Amen.

('For the armed forces' from *A Prayer Book
for the Armed Services*)

## 3.25 For more military chaplains

O Lord Jesus Christ,
instil in the hearts of priests
the desire to dedicate their lives to you as
    chaplains
to our Armed Forces.
Give courage and compassion
to those who serve you as Forces chaplains.

May their hearts be filled with zeal and love of
    you
so that your name may be better known and
    loved,
for you live and reign for ever and ever.

('Prayer for vocations to military chaplaincy'
from *The Armed Forces Simple Prayer Book*)

### 3.26 For the Women's Royal Army Corps

O merciful God and Father of us all, whose will it is that
we should help one another, give to us, the members
of the Women's Royal Army Corps, grace that we may
fulfil the same. Make us gentle, courteous and forbear-
ing. Direct our lives so that we may have courage and
resolution in the performance of our duty and hallow
all our friendships by the blessing of thy Spirit, for his
sake who loved us and gave himself for us, Jesus Christ
our Lord.                    (Historical Collect, 4 April 1955)

### 3.27 For those in transit

O Eternal Lord God, whose voice the raging seas
and the stormy winds obey; who in thy mercy guidest
the mariner in safety through the trackless deep;
Receive us, we beseech thee, into thy gracious and
Almighty protection. Preserve us from the perils of
the seas, from the danger of disease and from every

evil, that we may come in happiness and safety to the haven where we would be; through Jesus Christ our Lord. Amen.

('At sea' from *The Army Prayer Book, India*)

### 3.28 For the Airborne Forces

May the defence of the Most High be above and beneath, around and within us, in our going out and in our coming in, in our rising up and in our going down all our days and all our nights, until the dawn when the Son of Righteousness shall arise with healing in His wings for the people of the world, through Jesus Christ our Lord, Amen.

(Historical Collect, now the Collect of the Parachute Regiment)

### 3.29 Collect of the Royal Army Veterinary Corps

O God, who didst create man in thine own image, and gavest him dominion over every living thing, give wisdom and grace, we pray thee, to thy servants of the Royal Army Veterinary Corps, that we may guard these thy creatures committed to our care against disease and suffering and promote their health and usefulness; and may ever declare both by word and by example that the merciful man is kind to his beast, for his sake, who has told us that not one sparrow is forgotten before thee, Jesus Christ our merciful redeemer.                    (*Collects for the British Army*)

## 3.30 Collect of the Special Reconnaissance Regiment

Almighty God, whose Son Jesus Christ our Lord spoke of a master who commanded his servant, 'Go out into the highways and hedges and compel them to come in'; grant that we of the Special Reconnaissance Regiment, may, with your blessing, continue to operate concealed against the forces of evil in this world; guide us when we are alone, keep us always humble, resourceful and vigilant. Amen.

(Contemporary version of the regimental Collect)

## 3.31 For men in camp

Almighty God, our heavenly Father, visit, we pray thee, this Camp, its Commander, its Officers and Men, with thy love and favour. Strengthen us that we may be faithful in the performance of our duties; give us ready obedience and a love of discipline. Deliver us from loneliness and guard us in our temptations. Grant that we may have an abiding sense of thy presence; Increase in us true religion and of thy great mercy keep us in the same, through Jesus Christ, thine only Son our Lord. Amen.    (*A Prayer Book for Soldiers and Sailors*, 1917)

## 3.32  Collect of Queen Alexandra's Royal Army Nursing Corps

O God, who through the healing touch of thy dear Son didst recover the sick and relieve their pain, grant to us who serve beneath thy Cross in the Queen Alexandra's Royal Army Nursing Corps such love towards thee and devotion to our duty that the shadows may pass from those entrusted to our care, their darkness lighten into faith and hope, and thy love bring healing peace; for his sake who was content to suffer for all mankind, even Jesus Christ our Lord. Amen.

(Contemporary version of the Corps' Collect)

## 3.33  For the British armed forces

I pray this day for:
All members of the Armed Forces
currently serving overseas; at sea,
on land and in the air.

Those who have returned home injured
or maimed and those suffering in mind,
body or spirit.

Families, friends and military colleagues
grieving the loss of one who has died
on active service.

Those in the Armed Forces
whose task it is to use their professionalism
and skills in the service of our Sailors,
Marines, Soldiers, and Air Force personnel.

('Prayer pledge' from *The Armed Forces*
*Simple Prayer Book*)

### 3.34 Collect of the Corps of Royal Electrical and Mechanical Engineers

O God of power and might, whose all-pervading energy is the strength of nature and man, inspire, we pray Thee, us Thy servants of the Royal Electrical and Mechanical Engineers with the quickening spirit of goodwill, that as honest craftsmen, seeking only the good of all in peace or war, we may glorify Thee both in the work of our hands and in the example of our fellowship through Jesus Christ our Lord.

(Historical version of the Corps' Collect)

### 3.35 For the Counter IED Task Force

O God the giver of all good things and protector of those who put their trust in thee; look mercifully on members of the Counter IED Task Force as they protect and prepare the way; that serving thee with a quiet mind, they may find what is hidden and in darkness, defeat the devices and desires of the enemy, and be defended and comforted in all dangers and adversities.

> (Contemporary prayer from the Afghan
> conflict by Padre Andrew Earl)

### 3.36 For all in the armed forces

O Almighty God, we pray thy blessing upon us, whom thou hast joined together in the service of our country. Grant that we may so work and play, think and pray together, that we may be more perfectly fitted to serve thee also in the work to which thou hast called us. Help us to look wide, fill us with high ideals, inspire us with love and goodwill to all mankind that we may rightly lead our brethren into the paths of chivalry and honour, ourselves following in the steps of Him who died in the service of man, thy Son, our Saviour, Jesus Christ. Amen.

> ('For all in the forces' from *Divine Service
> Book for the Armed Forces*)

### 3.37 Collect of the Royal Gurkha Rifles

Almighty God, Father of all, whose ancient people looked to the hills, grant to us of the Brigade of Gurkhas, bound together in a bond of friendship, that we may serve our Sovereign with loyalty, integrity and cheerfulness; and mindful of our traditions, may we

thee follow wherever you lead, and so at the last come
to our eternal home, for the sake of him who called
his disciples his friends, even Jesus Christ our Lord.
Amen.

(Contemporary version of the regimental Collect)

### 3.38 A soldier's prayer in the midst of war

Stay with me God,
the night is dark, the night is cold,
my little spark of courage dies.
The night is long,
be with me God and make me strong.

I love a game, I love a fight.
I hate the dark, I love the light.
I love my child, I love my wife.
I am no coward, I love life.
Life, with its change of mood and shade,
I want to live, I'm not afraid,
but me and mine are hard to part,
Oh, unknown God, lift up my heart.

You stilled the waters at Dunkirk,
and saved your servants. All your work
is wonderful, dear God.
You strode before us down that dreadful road.
We were alone and hope had fled,

we loved our country and our dead,
and could not shame them,
so we stayed the course and were not much afraid.

Dear God, that nightmare road!
and then that sea!
We got there – we were men.
My eyes were blind, my feet were torn,
my soul sang like a bird at dawn!
I knew that death is but a door.
I knew what we were fighting for.
Peace for the kids, our brothers freed,
a kinder world, a cleaner breed.

I'm but the son my mother bore,
a simple man and nothing more.
But God of strength and gentleness,
be pleased to make me nothing less.
Help me, oh God, when death is near,
to mock the haggard face of fear,
that when I fall – if fall I must,
my soul may triumph in the dust.

(Anon, unpublished Second World
War soldier's prayer)

# 4

*Smoke clouds enwrap me
and cannons are crashing . . .*

## Prayers in the midst of war

What place is there for prayer in the midst of war? How is it possible speak to the God of love, with integrity, while engaged in combat? For some military personnel it proves impossible. Somewhere on the battlefield they lose the capacity to pray, their spiritual lives stifled by the clamour and the killing. Some stop praying because the language of faith has become meaningless, because it no longer seems to make sense to speak of a God of justice and forgiveness, of compassion and mercy in the midst of bloody carnage. Others stop praying when they hear no answer to their prayers, and in this silence come to question the presence – if not the very existence – of an all-loving God.

But prayer is not always a casualty of war. Some continue to call out to God from the battlefield, echoing the psalmist in their persistent demands for divine intervention, for redemption and justice. Others are driven to prayer by the very sights and experiences that cause others to lose their faith. To these Christians, the horrors of war are not proof of God's absence, but rather evidence of humanity's moral and emotional failings. Faced with these reminders of human limitation, they turn to God seeking personal forgiveness and a global change of heart.

## 4.1 In time of war

O Lord God, of infinite mercy, we beseech thee to look in compassion upon our country now involved in war. Pardon our offences, our pride and arrogance, our self-sufficiency and forgetfulness of thee. Give wisdom to our counsellors, skill to our officers, courage and endurance to our sailors, soldiers, and airmen, and all who guard our shores. Look in mercy on those immediately exposed to peril, to conflict, sickness, and death. Be with the dying; give to them true repentance and unfeigned trust in thee; and in the day of judgement, good Lord, deliver them. Finally, we beseech thee to remove in thy good providence all causes and occasions of war; to dispose our hearts and the hearts of our enemies to moderation; and of thy great goodness, to restore peace among the nations; through Christ our Lord. Amen.

> ('A prayer in time of war' from *Divine Service Book for the Armed Forces*)

## 4.2 For the British Empire during wartime

O God, who hast knit together our Empire in a new and closer unity by the spontaneous loyalty of its peoples: strengthen, deepen and purify that unity, that the Empire in its length and breadth may be filled with mercy and truth, righteousness and peace, and may seek thy glory and thy Kingdom; through Jesus Christ our Lord. Amen.

> ('For the British Empire' from *The Army Prayer Book, India*)

## 4.3 For allies in wartime

O Almighty Lord, who art a most strong tower to all those who put their trust in thee, to whom all things in heaven, in earth, and under the earth do bow and obey; Be now and evermore our defence; direct and prosper the cause of our country and of our Allies. May the kingdoms of this world, the kingdoms of all human authority, ambition, enterprise, and genius, become the kingdoms of our God. May rulers, presidents, and kings serve thee, the King of kings. In all parliaments and congresses may the divine ideals of justice, truth, and peace be had in honour; and stablish all in permanent fraternity, to thy great glory. Hear us, we beseech thee, through the mediation of thy Son, Jesus Christ our Lord. Amen.

> ('For the allied nations' from *A Prayer Book for Soldiers and Sailors*, 1917)

## 4.4 For the nation at war

Almighty God, King of Kings, God of battles, Prince of Peace, and Father of all men, we humbly beseech Thee to bless our most gracious sovereign King George and all the members of the royal family. Grant also to all who exercise authority under him in the State and hold command in his forces on land and sea, wisdom to devise and courage to carry out plans requisite for the establishment of peace on earth, amongst men of goodwill.

Hear our prayer for the safety of our comrades in arms in the Navy, Army, and Air Force, both of our King and his allies. Give them cheerfulness in enduring hardships, succour such as are in peculiar peril, bestow patience and ease on those in pain of body or anguish of spirit, grant success to the ministration of physicians and nurses for the sick and the wounded, and let the sorrowful sighing of the prisoner come before Thee.

Guard, sustain and comfort our loved ones at home. Forgive our enemies and turn their hearts, relieve those whose lands and goods are laid waste and destroyed by pitiless war, and through all the evils of the time accomplish Thine own unchangeable purpose to establish upon earth the Kingdom of our Lord and of His Christ; through the same Jesus Christ, our Mediator and Redeemer. Amen.

('General intercession' from *Service Hymn Book*)

## 4.5 A wartime prayer

O God, who makest wars to cease, crushing by the might of Thy strong defence the foes of them that put their trust in Thee; succour us Thy servants, who entreat Thy mercy, and break down the savage power of our enemies, that with unceasing thankfulness we may give praise to Thee.

O God, the Sovereign Lord of kingdoms and of kings, who in chastening dost heal, and in forgiving save; show forth upon us Thy mercy and restore to us the quiet times of peace, that we may make use of them to our amendment. Through our Lord Jesus Christ, Thy Son, who liveth and reigneth in the unity of the Holy Ghost, God, world without end. Amen.

('Prayers in time of war' from
*A Simple Prayer Book for Soldiers*)

### 4.6 Prayer for sailors and soldiers on active service

O Lord God of Hosts! Thou art our refuge and strength at all times. Unto thee we pour forth our hearts in prayer, that thou mayest be with us both in time of peace and of war, and shield us from all sorrow and hurt. Fill our hearts with courage and steadfastness that we may perform our duty to our King and Country for the honour of Israel and of the Empire. Do thou gird us with victory so that peace may speedily reign over all the earth. Into thy hands we commend our lives, for thou art our guardian and our deliverer. Amen!

(*Prayer Book for Jewish Sailors and Soldiers*)

### 4.7 For those protecting the nation

Almighty God, grant we pray Thee, that we who have been called to bear arms in the Service of our Country, whether on the sea, on the earth, or in the air, may be enabled to do so in a manner becoming good soldiers of Jesus Christ. Help us steadfastly to walk with Thee. Give us grace we beseech Thee, to be loyal to our Sovereign and valiant for our country: impart to us strength for the endurance of toil and hardship: indue us with courage and arm us with true valor, to resist the temptations to which we are exposed.

Above all, do Thou give us strength to subdue the
enemies of our own souls and bestow upon us grace
always to put our trust in Thee as our sure refuge and
defence. Amen.

('A prayer for the forces of the King' from
*Order of Divine Service for the CASF*)

## 4.8 Thanksgiving for comrades

Good God, I give thanks
for the courage of these brothers and sisters in arms.
For the strength of their backs and their wills,
for their grit and their trustiness,
for their spirit and determination,
for their sense and their skill,
I give you thanks.
May I be to them as good a comrade
as they have been to me,
and may your strong arm defend and empower us
    daily.
Amen.

(Jennifer Phillips in *A Prayer Book for
the Armed Services*)

## 4.9 St Patrick's Breastplate

May the strength of God support us;
May the power of God preserve us;

May the wisdom of God instruct us;
May the hand of God protect us;
May the way of God direct us;
May the shield of God defend us;
May the host of God guard us against the snares
    of evil
and the temptations of the world;
May Christ be with us, Christ before us,
Christ in us, Christ over us.
May thy salvation, O Lord, be always ours,
this day and for evermore. Amen.

(Traditional Christian prayer from
*Pray with the Navy*)

## 4.10 King Alfred's prayer

Lord God Almighty,
we pray thee for thy great mercy to guide us to
    thy will,
to make our minds steadfast,
to strengthen us against temptation,
to put all evil far from us.
Shield us against our foes, seen and unseen;
teach us that we may inwardly love thee
before all things with a clean mind and a clean body;
for thou art our Maker and Redeemer,
our help and our strength,

our trust and our hope,
now and for ever. Amen.

(Historical Christian prayer from *Refuge and Strength*)

## 4.11  For strength of character

God, give me strength to run this race,
God, give me power to do the right,
And courage lasting through the fight;
God give me strength to see your face,
And heart to stand till evil cease,
And at the last, O God, your peace. Amen.

*(Pray with the Navy)*

## 4.12  On the march

Stretch out Thine hand, O Lord, to me, Thine unworthy servant, and so direct my steps, that, walking
always in the way of Thy commandments, I fail not
finally to attain to everlasting life. Suffer not weariness
to overmaster me, nor trouble or anxiety to cast me
down; but be Thou my stronghold and my deliverer,
my rock of defence, to which I may always flee; and
when the march of time is over, accept me in eternity,
for the sake of Jesus Christ, my Lord and my Redeemer.
Amen.

(G. R. Gleig, Chaplain-General,
*The Soldier's Manual of Devotion*)

## 4.13 On sentry duty

O Thou, whose eyes are everywhere, beholding the evil and the good, watch over me, and over my comrades now and evermore. Make us vigilant and sober, earnest and true, that no enemy may surprise us, either in our bodies or our souls. Amid the darkness of night give us faith to behold Thee; and under the burning noon refresh us with Thy favour. And when at last life's warfare comes to an end, receive us into some one of the mansions of Thy house in Heaven, for Jesus Christ's sake, our Lord and Saviour. Amen.

('On picket' from G. R. Gleig, Chaplain-General,
*The Soldier's Manual of Devotion*)

## 4.14 For perseverance

Teach us, Good Lord,
to serve Thee as Thou deservest;
To give and not to count the cost;
To fight and not to heed the wounds;
To toil and not to seek for rest;
To labour and to look for no reward,
save that of knowing that we do Thy will.
Amen.

('Prayer of St Ignatius Loyola' from
*Commando Prayer Book*)

## 4.15  Sir Francis Drake's prayer

O Lord, when thou givest to thy servants to endeavour in any great matter, grant us also to know that it is not the beginning but the continuing of the same until it be thoroughly finished that yieldeth the true glory, through Him who for the finishing of thy work laid down his life, Jesus Christ our Lord. Amen.

(Prayer traditionally attributed to Sir Francis Drake from *Pray with the Navy*)

## 4.16  Montgomery's prayer

'We must not forget to give thanks to the Lord, "mighty in battle", for giving us such a good beginning towards the attainment of our object . . . And now let us get on with the job. Together with our American Allies, we have knocked Mussolini off his perch. We will now drive the Germans from Sicily.'

('General Montgomery gives thanks', 1943, from *Prayers and Graces*)

## 4.17  For victory

O Lord, who sufferest not Thy servants to be tempted above they are able, and givest power to the faint, vouchsafe to be our strength and comfort in this our time of trial, prepare us for all that may befall us, gird us with Thy whole armour, enable us to play the man for Thee and for the cities of our God, and if it please Thee give to our righteous cause good success; through Jesus Christ our Lord. Amen.    (*Service Hymn Book*)

## 4.18 For freedom and justice

Almighty God, give us grace fearlessly to fight against evil, and to make no peace with oppression. Grant that we may use our freedom to maintain justice among all people and nations; to the glory of your holy Name; through Jesus Christ our Lord. Amen.

(*Armed Forces Operational Service and Prayer Book*)

## 4.19 For the defeat of evil designs

O God of battles, Who grantest the victory to those who put their trust in Thee; mercifully hear the prayers of us, Thy servants, that the evil designs of our enemies being defeated, we may praise Thee with unceasing gratitude. Amen.

('Prayer for victory' from
*Catholic Prayer Book for HM Forces*)

## 4.20 For the coming battle

O Lord God of Hosts, who willest that men should ever do their duty; I humbly confess my sins and claim thy loving mercy and forgiveness. Be thou with me in the hours of danger and help me to play the man. If it be thy good will, preserve me in safety, or else vouchsafe to receive me into everlasting life; through Jesus Christ our Lord. Amen.

(*The Army Prayer Book, India*)

## 4.21 For grace to die well

O God, who holdest our souls in life, and hast appointed unto all men once to die; Grant that when our last hour cometh, we may not be dismayed; but may commend our spirits to Thy care; trusting in the merits of Thy Son our Savior. And this we beg for the sake of Him who died for us that we might live with Thee forever. Amen.

('For grace to die' from *Service Prayer Book*)

## 4.22 Lord Robert's prayer

Almighty Father, I have often sinned against Thee. O wash me in the precious blood of the Lamb of God. Fill me with Thy Holy Spirit that I may lead a new life. Spare me to see again those whom I love at home, or fit me for Thy presence in peace. Strengthen us to quit ourselves like men in our righteous cause. Keep us faithful unto death, calm in danger, patient in suffering, merciful as well as brave – true to our country and our colours. If it be Thy will, enable us to win the victory for human liberty; but above all grant us the better victory over temptation and sin – over life and death that we may be more than conquerors through Him who loved us and laid down His life for us – Jesus Christ our Savior, the Captain of the army of God. Amen.

(Traditional Christian prayer from
*Service Prayer Book*)

## 4.23 Patton's Third Army prayer

Almighty and most merciful Father, we humbly beseech thee, of thy great goodness, to restrain these immoderate rains with which we have had to contend. Grant us fair weather for battle. Graciously hearken to us as soldiers who call thee that, armed with thy power, we may advance from victory to victory, and crush the oppression and wickedness of our enemies, and establish thy justice among men and nations. Amen.

(James H. O'Neill, Senior Chaplain, 3rd Army,
8 December 1944, written in response to General
Patton's instructions, from *Refuge and Strength*)

## 4.24 Nelson's prayer

May the great God, whom I worship, grant to my country and for the benefit of Europe in general, a great and glorious victory: and may no misconduct, in any one, tarnish it: and may humanity after victory be the predominant feature in the British fleet. For myself individually, I commit my life to Him who made me and may His blessing light upon my endeavours for serving my country faithfully. To Him I resign myself and the just cause which is entrusted to me to defend. Amen. Amen. Amen.

(Written on the eve of the Battle of Trafalgar, 1805, from *The Naval Church Service Book, Leader's Copy*)

## 4.25 For courage in battle

Almighty God, Father of our Lord Jesus Christ, the guardian, sustainer and guide of all who put their trust in you, grant us the power of your Holy Spirit that we may always live up to what we are called to be. Grant us the gifts of inward vision, determination, and strength that we may approach the varied duties, tasks and dangers ahead of us with faith, with confidence and with courage and thus in all things be more than conquerors through Jesus Christ our Lord. Amen.

(*Armed Forces Operational Service and Prayer Book*)

## 4.26 For the day of battle

Lord, help me today to realize that you will be speaking to me through the events of the day, through people, through things and through all creation. Give me ears, eyes and heart to perceive you, however veiled your presence may be. Give me insight to see through the exterior of things to the interior truth. Give me your Spirit of discernment. O Lord, you know how busy I must be this day. If I forget you, do not forget me. Amen.

('A prayer on the day of battle' by Jacob Astley, before the Battle of Edgehill, 1642, from *Commando Prayer Book*)

## 4.27 Before going into battle

Almighty God, and heavenly Father, enter not into judgment with Thy servant, but for the sake of Jesus Christ forgive the sins of my past life, though they be many. Enable me this day to do my duty. And, if it be Thy good pleasure, bring me safe and unhurt out of all the dangers which beset me. Or, should Thy wisdom order otherwise, and wounds or death be my appointed portion, make me submissive to Thy will; and in the end take me to Thyself, washed in the blood of Him who died for our sins, and rose again for our justification, Jesus Christ our Lord. Amen.

(G. R. Gleig, Chaplain-General, *The Soldier's Manual of Devotion*)

## 4.28 For those going into battle

Almighty God, look down in mercy upon us, Thine unworthy servants, who come unto Thee in prayer, asking Thee to go forth with us now, making us fit for every duty, and upholding us by Thine almighty power.

Teach our hands to war; make our arms strong; and gird us with might in the battle. Deliver us, if it be Thy will, from wounds and death, and grant us the victory. Remove fear far from us, and enable us to quit ourselves like men. Prosper the just cause, O God, and bring us forth in safety from the midst of our enemies. Then will we give thanks unto Thee, O Lord, and will sing praises unto Thy name.

Bless all our dear ones in distant lands. Keep them and do them good, O God of our salvation; and, if it be Thy holy will, spare us to join them again in the land of our birth; but above all, grant to every one of us such faith and true holiness that, through Jesus our Lord, we may come at last into Thy heavenly kingdom. O God, keep us all faithful unto death; and then do Thou give unto us the crown of life. Amen.

('Before a battle' from *The Scottish Service Book*)

## 4.29 Before a battle at sea

O most powerful and glorious Lord God, the Lord of hosts, that rulest and commandest all things; Thou sittest in the throne judging right, and therefore we make our address to Thy Divine Majesty in this our necessity, that Thou wouldest take the cause into Thine Own hand, and judge between us and our enemies. Stir up Thy strength, O Lord, and come and help us; for Thou givest not always the battle to the strong, but canst save by many or by few. O let not our sins now cry against us for vengeance; but hear us, Thy poor servants, begging mercy and imploring Thy help, and that Thou wouldest be a defence unto us against the face of the enemy. Make it appear that Thou art our Saviour and mighty Deliverer, through Jesus Christ our Lord. Amen.

('The prayer to be said before a fight at sea against any enemy' from *Service Prayer Book*)

### 4.30 For divine protection

Novena: O Jesus, I have come to beg your help. Heart of Jesus, save France. Protect us from German bullets. Joan of Arc, save us. Saint Michael, pray for us. This prayer was sent to me and must be circulated throughout the front. It is said that those who write it will be preserved from all calamities and those who neglect it will have bad luck. Send it to nine different people one each day and on the ninth day you will receive great joy. Do not sign it, only give the date you received it. Do not break the chain, have faith. 9/8/15.

(French 'Chain-prayer', 1915, from *War and Faith*)

## 4.31 In the face of fear

Lord, in the garden of Gethsemane
you shared with everyone who has ever been afraid.
You conquered fear with love
and returned saying, 'Do not be afraid!'
In the light of your love,
death has lost its sting and so has fear.
Lord, may your love be the key that releases me
    from fear.
Amen.                                    (*Pray with the Navy*)

## 4.32 For rest in the midst of turmoil

O God, my refuge and strength: in this place of unrelent-
ing light and noise, enfold me in your holy darkness
and silence, that I may rest secure under the shadow
of your wings. Amen.

    ('For rest' from *A Prayer Book for the Armed Services*)

## 4.33 Special prayers in the face of the enemy

Thou, O Lord, art just and powerful:
    O defend our cause against the face of the enemy.
O God, Thou art a strong tower of defense to all
    who fly unto Thee:
    O save us from the violence of the enemy.
O Lord of hosts, fight for us, that we may glorify
    Thee.

O suffer us not to sink under the weight of our
sins, or the violence of the enemy.

O Lord, arise, help us, and deliver us for Thy name's
sake. Amen.                    (*Service Prayer Book*)

## 4.34 For protection from firearms

Prayer to protect against firearms. As a counter-charm,
recite this prayer three times in succession every morning before breakfast, wear it and you will be preserved
from all peril and danger of death, and you will always
overcome your enemies. Prayer. Eccé, Crucem, domini,
fugité, partès, adversé, vicis, l'eodé, Tribu, Juda, make
the sign of the cross, radix, clavo.

> (French prayer card, First World War,
> from *War and Faith*)

## 4.35 For divine aid

O God, who art the author of peace and lover of
concord, in knowledge of whom standeth our eternal
life, whose service is perfect freedom; Defend us thy
humble servants in all assaults of our enemies; that
we, surely trusting in thy defence, may not fear the
power of any adversaries, through the might of Jesus
Christ our Lord. Amen.

> (*The Second Collect, For Peace* from *A Form
> of Prayer for Open Air Services*, 1902)

## 4.36 In the midst of battle

Father, I call Thee!
Smoke clouds enwrap me and cannons are crashing,
Round me the terrible lightnings are flashing.
Guide of all battles, I call Thee!
Father, oh guide me!

Father, oh guide me!
Guide me to victory and to death lead me:
Lord, Thy commandments I know and I heed Thee;
Lord, as Thou willest, so guide me!
My God, I heed Thee!

My God, I heed Thee!
Once amid murmur of leaves I could hear Thee,
Now in the thunder of war I am near Thee.
Fountain of mercy, I heed Thee.
Father, oh bless me!

Father, oh bless me!
Into Thy hand my life I surrender:
Thou hast bestowed it, so take it, Defender!
Living or dying, oh bless me!
Father, I praise Thee!

Father, I praise Thee!
Not for the goods of this earth we are fighting:

To guard the holiest, our swords are smiting.
Falling in triumph, I praise Thee.
My God, I trust Thee! `

My God, I trust Thee!
When all the thunders of death are roaring,
When from my veins the blood is pouring:
My life, God, I trust to Thee!
Father, I call Thee!

(Theodor Körner, 1791, in
*A Harvest of German Verse*)

# 5

## *Let thy Holy Angels encamp around this place . . .*

### Prayers from the home front

Wars are not only fought by the armed forces but by a whole country. Every time a nation engages in military action, it has physical, economic, moral and spiritual implications for itself as well as for the enemy. The material effects are obvious, but the non-physical results are equally real. Wars can leave a people culturally wounded: spiritually traumatized, emotionally scarred and morally insolvent.

In the short term, in the immediate aftermath of a war, these wounds can have a profound effect upon a nation's decisions and global interactions. But they can also have a much longer-term effect. Wars create a new chapter in the national narrative, one that in the telling can have implications for generations to come. In this sense, wars can change the way a people view themselves and are viewed by others. In addition, if left unaddressed, cultural wounds can fester. In the worst of cases, prolonged, bitter conflicts can result in a form of 'cultural disfigurement' where a nation's identity, values, beliefs and traditions are permanently lost.

At a personal level, the cost of war is not felt principally by its staff officers or politicians, but by the families of those who have died. Every man or woman who marches to war leaves a family behind, and every death leaves a void in these families. At this level, every single one of our war dead has truly changed history – not necessarily world history as we understand it played out on the global stage, but history as it enfolds quietly and often unseen, history at a very personal, local level. Each war death alters family relations and community dynamics. And from there, who knows? What effect can one death have on a world? Within the Christian faith we are well aware of the answer.

The majority of prayers in this section are British, dating back to the First and Second World Wars. From them we gain some insight into the spiritual life of a nation at war. Many of the prayers express concern for the welfare of the armed forces. Some focus on the needs of refugees and evacuees, the enemy and prisoners of war, while others commend the myriad of workers labouring on the home front; those factory workers, doctors, miners and writers each of whom made their own unique contribution to the war effort. Collectively, these British prayers represent another facet of the nation's history: they illustrate the spiritual component of a country caught up in the turmoil of global conflict.

## 5.1 On the declaration of war

O Lord God of Hosts! thou art our refuge and strength, a very present help in trouble. With anxious minds and trembling hearts we approach thee to-day in prayer and supplication. Kingdoms shake and nations tremble. The shout of the warrior and the roar of battle resound to the ends of the earth because of the fury of the oppressor. The terrors of war are upon us; they have come close to our gates.

Yet we will not fear. Thou, who searchest the hearts of men and knowest the innermost thoughts of rulers, wilt judge our cause. Our fathers trusted in thee and thou didst deliver them. To thee alone our eyes are lifted up, who bringest low the haughty and protectest the upright in spirit. With thine own wisdom direct the rulers and counsellors of our nation. Gird our hosts with strength and courage and victory on land and on sea. Keep thou far from us pestilence and famine; and shield our homes from sorrow and hurt.

Our Father, our King! hearken unto our cry; save us for thy name's sake, so that loyalty and faithfulness be indeed the stability of our times. Speedily cause righteousness to triumph and the lovers of justice to rejoice; and hasten the day when thy tabernacle of peace shall be spread over all the children of men for evermore. Amen.

(Prayer composed by the Chief Rabbi on
the declaration of war, August 1914, from
*Prayer Book for Jewish Sailors and Soldiers*)

## 5.2  For the nation at the onset of war

O Lord God, we beseech Thee to be with us in this hour of crisis. Strengthen our King; give guidance to our rulers; uphold our soldiers, sailors and airmen, that with courage, endurance, and self-restraint they may meet whatever trials they may be called upon to face. May we as a nation carry on this war without bitterness or self-seeking, not shrinking from what sacrifices may be required of us, desiring only that Thy ways may be established among men, and that the safety, honour, and welfare of our country may be assured. Bless and uphold our ally. May the hearts of men everywhere turn to Thee for help, so that even this dark hour may hasten the coming of Thy Kingdom, and reveal Thee afresh to the world. Make us strong

in the faith that Thou wilt defend the right, and grant
us quickly an abiding peace. Through Jesus Christ our
Lord. Amen. (*Per Christum Vinces*)

## 5.3 Giving thanks in the midst of war

Let us give thanks:

For the grace given us as a nation to champion the right,
and to suffer and endure.

For the courage and endurance of our sailors, soldiers,
and airmen

in face of hardship and danger.

For the courage and service of our fishermen and
seamen,

on the deep waters and exposed to the snares and
assaults of the enemy.

For the splendid response of the men of our own land
and of the Dominions across the seas to the call of
King and country.

For the noble response of the women of our land
in national service.

For the awakening of many to the serious issues of
life and of death.

For the full sufficiency of Christ and His Gospel
to meet every need of human souls,
and to bring healing to the nations. Amen.

(A. R. Howell, *Church Prayers for War-Time*)

## 5.4 For divine protection for the nation

Our Father in Heaven, we beseech Thee of Thy great mercy to give Thine Angels charge over our high seas. Grant Thy Divine protection to all our seaside towns, and the villages on the coast. Save our mariners and all who travel by water from the dangers of submarines, and hidden mines. Protect our airmen from tempests and from hidden foes. Spare our Fatherland from the ravages of invasion by air, the landing of hostile armies, and the treachery of spies. Let Thy Holy Angels encamp around this place, and the habitations of those near and dear to us. Speedily restore if it may be, peace in this greatly troubled world. We ask it in the name of the Prince of Peace. Amen.

*(Per Christum Vinces)*

## 5.5 For Britain and her allies

O Almighty Lord, who art a most strong tower to all them that put their trust in thee, to whom all things in heaven, in earth, and under the earth, do bow and obey: Be now and evermore our defence; prosper the forces of our King and his Allies; decide the issues of this war according to righteousness; have mercy on all the wounded, our own and of the enemy; succour the dying; comfort the bereaved; cheer the anxious; uphold the faith of thy servants, and give peace and lasting concord. Hear us, O Lord, from heaven thy dwelling-place, and when thou hearest, forgive; through the mediation of thy Son, Jesus Christ our Lord. Amen.

(John Taylor Smith, Chaplain-General, 'Prayer for ourselves and our allies' from *The War*)

## 5.6 For the allied nations

Let thy merciful loving-kindness, most gracious Father, bring comfort and strength to the nations of Poland, France, Czecho-Slovakia, Norway, Holland and Belgium; heal their wounds; console their mourners; support their sufferers; and grant to our nation both the will and the wisdom truly to share the burden of their griefs for the sake of our Redeemer, Jesus Christ.

('For our allies', adapted in *Prayers in Time of War*)

## 5.7 Intercessions for other nations

*Lord, hear our prayer*
*And let our cry come unto Thee.*

Let us remember before God the people of Poland, cruelly wronged, pledging ourselves to give what help we can, and praying for their eventual liberation and independence.

Let us pray for the Czechs, living under daily fear and humiliation, that they may be patient in the day of affliction and merciful in the day of triumph.

Let us pray for Jewish and non-Aryan refugees and all who have been cast out of the community of National Socialist Germany; and let us especially remember those now in internment camps in this country.

Let us in our prayers join ourselves in spirit to our Christian brethren in Germany, and especially those who are suffering imprisonment for their faith. Let us give thanks to God for the courageous example of men like Martin Niemöller and pray that we may be worthy to be numbered among the company of Thy heroes.                    (*Per Christum Vinces*)

## 5.8 For the enemy

O God, whose love goes out to all thy children, we thank thee for the multitude of men and women in Germany in whose hearts peace and goodwill prevail, who have loved us, and whom we have loved, fellow members with us in the Church of Christ, and fellow servants of his Kingdom. Side by side with them, we kneel to-day and beg of thee that thou wilt send us thy peace.

Deliver them and us from any spirit of personal hatred. Take away the causes of bitter misunderstanding between us. Strengthen among them and among us all who seek thy reign of justice, fair dealing and love. We ask it in the name of our one Lord, Jesus Christ.

(Hugh Martin in *Prayers in Time of War*)

## 5.9 For the armed forces

Almighty God, we commend to Thee our protecting armies, who on land and sea, and beneath the sea and in the air, give their lives to be our shield of defence. Accept their sacrifice, that the dread work they are called to do may have a right issue in liberating the world from the tyranny of force, and enabling the advent of a freedom formed of righteousness and peace; through Him Who died to witness to Thy truth, Jesus Christ our Lord, Who liveth and reigneth with Thee in the unity of the Holy Ghost, one God, world without end. Amen.

(Father Andrew SDC, 'For the forces' from
*Prayers for Use in War-Time*)

## 5.10 Mid-day Prayer

O God, guard and bless our sailors and soldiers, and give us victory and peace. Amen.

(John Taylor Smith, Chaplain-General, *The War*)

## 5.11  For our armed forces

Almighty God, the protector of all, be with those in our Armed Forces who face danger. Grant them courage and professionalism in the tasks which they are called to undertake that they may always forward the cause of peace and security in our nation and in our world; through Jesus Christ your Son our Lord. Amen.

> (Contemporary civilian church prayer from Rhydybriw Chapel of Ease, Sennybridge Training Camp)

## 5.12  For our Navy and Army

O Almighty Lord God, King of kings, and Governor of all things, that sitteth in the throne judging right; We commend to thy Fatherly goodness the men who, as sailors or soldiers, are serving our Empire on sea or land in the war, beseeching thee to take into thine own hand both them and the cause for which they are fighting. Be thou their tower of strength in the midst of the dangers of earthly warfare. Make all bold through death or life to put their trust in thee, who art the only giver of all victory, and canst save by many or by few; through Jesus Christ our Lord. Amen.

> (John Taylor Smith, Chaplain-General, *The War*)

## 5.13 For those wounded in action

Lord God, we pray for those in our Armed Forces who are injured in the course of their duty. May they receive the best of all care, both bodily and mentally, that they may be enabled to live as full a life as possible and that they may know that society both values and honours them; through our Saviour Jesus Christ. Amen.

(Contemporary civilian church prayer from Rhydybriw Chapel of Ease, Sennybridge Training Camp)

## 5.14 For the sailors of our fleet

O Thou that slumberest not nor sleepest, protect, we pray thee, our Sailors from the hidden perils of the sea, from the snares and assaults of the enemy. In the anxious hours of waiting, steady and support those on whom the burdens of responsibility lie heavily, and grant that in dangers often, in watchings often, in weariness often, they may serve thee with a quiet mind; through Jesus Christ our Lord. Amen.

(John Taylor Smith, Chaplain-General, *The War*)

## 5.15 For prisoners of war

O Lord Almighty, Father of mercies, Friend to all who are comfortless and forlorn, we pray Thee to consider with especial loving-kindness all who are captives of war, and in the hands of the enemy. Thou, who art present everywhere and in all things, make Thy presence such to them that in the weariness and unrest of their imprisonment they may find spiritual freedom in Thee, being released from fears and from sins, from darkness and oppression of the heart, from bitterness of hope deferred. Lead them thus onward in divine knowledge in their school of trial, and in Thy mercy speed the day of righteous peace and of their glad deliverance. All this we humbly ask in the Name of Him who gave Himself for our eternal freedom, Thy dear Son, Jesus Christ our Lord. Amen.

(*Per Christum Vinces*)

## 5.16 For those providing national service

Our Father, in these hours of daylight we remember those who must wake that we may sleep; bless those who watch over us at night, the firemen and police, the air raid wardens, and all who carry on through the hours of darkness the restless commerce of men on land and sea. We thank thee for their faithfulness and sense of duty: we pray thee for pardon if our selfishness or luxury adds to their nightly toil. Grant that we may realise how dependent

the safety of our loved ones and the comforts of
life are on these our brothers, that so we may think
of them with love and gratitude and help to make
their burden lighter; for the sake of Jesus Christ
our Lord.

> (Walter Rauschenbusch, 'National service',
> adapted in *Prayers in Time of War*)

### 5.17 For the home services

O Lord Jesu Christ, who hast taught us by Thy word
and example that the perfect friendship is shown
in sacrifice, we ask for Thy blessing and protection
for all those who are ready to lay down their lives
for their friends in fighting the flames of fire, and
standing up against the attacks of the enemy upon
our homes: Who livest and reignest with the Father
and the Holy Spirit, One God, world without end.
Amen.

> (Father Andrew SDC, in *Prayers for Use
> in War-Time*)

### 5.18 For industry and commerce

O Blessed Saviour, who wast pleased Thyself to labour
among men as the Son of Man: Have mercy, we
pray Thee upon those who labour now in factories
or workshops for the service of their country; guard

them in all dangers; preserve them in all temptations; and grant them such health of mind and body that they may serve their brethren faithfully and well, and do the things that are pleasing unto Thee; who livest and reignest with the Father and the Holy Spirit, ever one God, world without end. Amen.

(*Per Christum Vinces*)

## 5.19 For all in society

O God, who hast given all men their work to do, help them to do it with all their might. Give wisdom to the King and all who govern us. Bless the men and women who work in offices and factories. Give strength to those who work hard at the docks or in the fields. Take care of the miners and sailors, and all whose work is dangerous. Watch over the children who are at school preparing for their work; and help us all to follow in the steps of him who worked as a carpenter, Jesus Christ our Lord.

('The challenge' from *Prayers in Time of War*)

## 5.20 For those who provide the nation's food

Almighty God, our Heavenly Father, we Thy children come to Thee in this our time of need. We thank Thee that for so many years Thou hast preserved us from anxiety about our food, and we pray that Thou wilt, in Thy mercy, help us in this time of scarcity. Make us unselfish and considerate of the needs of others, and careful and prudent in our own use of food. Guard and protect we humbly pray Thee, our merchant ships and those of our ally, and of the neutral nations, save them from their secret enemies and from every peril of the seas. Bless, we pray Thee, the labours of all who are sowing and planting for the common good, and we beseech Thee grant such weather as may bring forth the fruits of the earth in due season, for Thou alone canst give the increase. We ask it for Jesus Christ's sake. Amen.

*(Per Christum Vinces)*

## 5.21 For speakers and writers

Direct, O Lord, those who speak where many listen and write what many read; that they may do their part in making the heart of the people wise, its mind sound, its will righteous: to the honour of Jesus Christ our Lord.                    *(Prayers in Time of War)*

## 5.22 For doctors and nurses

Almighty Father, Creator of all life, Who gave Thy Son to be the Redeemer of the world, Who Himself bade us fulfil Thy law of love in bearing one another's burdens and came that we might have life more abundantly: Give to all doctors and nurses courage, skill and patience, that with sure hand and tender touch they may become ministers of Thy healing mercy; through Jesus Christ our Lord, Restorer and Healer of all things, who liveth and reigneth with Thee and the Holy Spirit, one God, world without end. Amen.

(Father Andrew SDC, *Prayers for Use in War-Time*)

## 5.23 For refugees

O God, our Father, who hast made of one blood all nations upon the earth, and called all mankind thy children: we pray for thy blessing upon all refugees who have sought safety and freedom in our land. Teach both them and us the secrets of true friendship. Let them not be lost in what is strange and bewildering to them here, and deliver us from any contempt, prejudice or misunderstanding, that may separate us from them. Help us to labour together to build a righteous society founded on brotherhood and justice. We ask this in the name of him who taught us to help the stranger and the alien, even Jesus Christ our Lord.

(Hugh Martin, *Prayers in Time of War*)

## 5.24 For those involved in the evacuation of children

O Lord Jesu, Who didst bid the weary come to Thee for rest, let Thy blessing be on all those who are receiving others into their homes: Grant that by mutual love those who welcome and those who come may find their lives enriched by a new experience of fellowship: Grant to the children contentment and protection, and to those who receive them the sympathy and understanding that alone can make a home: Who with the Father and the Holy Ghost livest for ever, One God, world without end. Amen.

(Father Andrew SDC, 'For those in reception areas' from *Prayers for Use in War-Time*)

## 5.25 For children during wartime

O Lord Jesu Christ, Who in Thy babyhood wast borne by Thy mother to Egypt for fear of a hostile king, we commend to Thy mercy all little children in poverty and pain or in exile from their homes, that Thou, the Good Shepherd, wouldst shield and shelter them in Thy love; Who livest and reignest with the Father in the unity of the Holy Spirit, one God, world without end. Amen.

(Father Andrew SDC, 'For children' from *Prayers for Use in War-Time*)

## 5.26 For evacuated children

O Blessed Jesus, Who in the days of thy flesh didst share the life of an earthly home, look down in mercy upon the children of our great cities who have been taken from their homes. May the families of which they are now members reveal to them the joy which fills a Christian home; sustain and comfort the parents from whom they are parted; strengthen and inspire their teachers and all who have charge of them; and when the war is over restore them to homes made safe by the victory of thy righteousness; we ask it for Thy Name's sake who art the Prince of Peace. Amen.

*(Per Christum Vinces)*

## 5.27 For evacuees

O Father in whose family all men are children, we remember before thee all homes broken by separation in this time of war. We pray for mothers and children divided from each other, for husbands and wives compelled to live apart, and especially for homes from which the husband, son or brother has gone to serve in the forces. Soften, we pray thee, these hard blows by the comfort of thy good Spirit. Be with the lonely. Help them to maintain the links that bind them to those they love. May fellowship in spirit be preserved, though bodily presence be denied. Teach us all that neither death nor life can separate us or ours from thy love which is in Jesus Christ our Lord.

(Hugh Martin, *Prayers in Time of War*)

## 5.28 For mothers

O Lord Jesus Christ, Whom Thy Father spared not that Thy Cross might be the supreme revelation of divine love, Whose blessed mother was allowed to stand beside Thy Cross and share Thy Passion: Give to all mothers, stricken by the death of their dear ones, such trust in Thee that even in the hour of darkness their souls may magnify Thy name, Who livest and reignest with the Father and the Holy Ghost for ever. Amen.

(Father Andrew SDC, *Prayers for Use in War-Time*)

## 5.29 For those in danger of temptation

Most merciful Father, have mercy, we beseech Thee, on all women who are tempted and in danger through loneliness. Defend them from bad companions. Grant them steadfastness and patience when they are excited and bewildered; preserve in them the spirit of gentleness and dignity; and give them such true friends that the enemy of souls may not

triumph over their weakness: through Jesus Christ
our Lord. Amen.                    (*Per Christum Vinces*)

## 5.30 A wartime grace

Upon this scanty meal, O Lord,
Bestow a blessing in accord:
Pour Thy grace in measure small,
Lest it more than cover all.

Bless the tiny piece of ham:
Bless the lonely dab of jam:
Bless the sparsely-buttered toast,
Father, Son and Holy Ghost.

('A benison on wartime high tea' from
*Prayers and Graces*)

## 5.31 For loved ones

O Lord our God, Who art in every place, and from
Whom no space or distance can ever separate us,
we know that those who are absent from each other
are still present with Thee. We therefore pray Thee
to have in Thy holy keeping those dear ones from
whom we are now separated, and grant that both
they and we, by drawing nearer unto Thee, may be
drawing nearer unto each other, bound together by
the unseen chain of Thy Love, in the Communion

of Thy Spirit, and in the Holy Fellowship of Thy Saints, that whether or not, according as it seems best to Thee, we meet again on earth, we may surely meet again at the Resurrection of the just, and go in together to that House of many Mansions which Thou hast prepared for them that unfeignedly love Thee; through Jesus Christ our Lord. Amen.

(*Per Christum Vinces*)

# 6

## *Stretch forth your wounded hands . . .*

### Prayers after the battle

War has a human cost. All too often this cost is paid by civilians, by those who are unfortunate enough to get caught between the warring parties. But sometimes, if society is lucky, the brunt of the cost will be paid by its military, by those who have signed up to do the job, who have been trained to do it well and who, on the whole, complain little when asked to fulfil their side of the military covenant.

But what of the price they pay? What cost does war extract from those men and women who are willing to put their lives on the line for their country, their families and their friends? There is no doubt that some people thrive on the battlefield. Some military personnel return from war with renewed confidence and a sense of satisfaction. This should not be mistaken for arrogance, bloodlust or a callous disregard for the dead. In many cases the opposite is true and their experiences of battle have convinced these veterans of the horrors of war. But in spite of this revelation, in spite of this recognition that war is at best the lesser of two evils, they still exude a certain pride. This is the pride common to all professionals who have done the job that they have been trained to do and who have performed to the best of their abilities. It is a pride natural to anyone who has been tested and not been found wanting.

But then there are the others, those who leave the battlefield not as confident conquerors, heroic warriors who have honed their skills in the fires of war, but as men and women who have been deeply debilitated by war, those who have been burned by the very fire that forged resilience in others. For some service personnel these wounds are physical, but in others they are much less obvious. Some return with psychological scars, with post-traumatic stress disorders or depression. Others bear soul-wounds, spiritual damage associated with feelings of shame or guilt, often accompanied by the sense that they have not always acted as they ought. If left untreated, these moral wounds can prove just as life-threatening as any shell or bullet.

Sometimes those who have survived the battle turn to God in prayer, speaking to God from the abyss, searching for comfort amid the human detritus. Too soon yet to ask grand metaphysical questions, those fresh from the battlefield offer prayers in which we see the expression of much more pressing needs: healing for the wounded, peace for the dying, and blessings for the dead.

## 6.1 When the battle is over

Almighty Father, who of Thy great mercy and goodness hast saved us in the day of battle and delivered us out of the hands of our enemies, we thankfully acknowledge Thy great goodness. May Thy grace enable us truly to thank Thee, and to devote to Thy service the lives which Thou hast spared. Because Thou hast been our help, therefore in the shadow of Thy wings will we rejoice. Because Thou hast delivered our souls from death, we will walk before Thee in the land of the living.

Continue to us, we beseech Thee, Thy protection, and teach us steadfastly to put our trust in Thee, so that we may not fear although an host encamp against us. Grant us Thine aid in our warfare, and crown our arms with victory, that peace may be restored; for the sake of Jesus Christ our Lord. Amen.

('After a battle' from *The Scottish Service Book*)

## 6.2 A prayer of thanksgiving

O Lord God, in whose hand is the life of everything, and the breath of all mankind; We magnify thy goodness in that thou hast been pleased to save from deadly hurt thy servant who now desireth (or for whom we desire) to offer thee the sacrifice of praise and thanksgiving. Give him grace, we humbly beseech thee, worthily to spend in thy service the days which thou hast so mercifully prolonged, that henceforth dwelling always under thy protection he may abide in thy love unto his life's end; through Jesus Christ our Saviour. Amen.

('A thanksgiving for an escape from a special peril' from *A Prayer Book for Soldiers and Sailors*, 1917)

## 6.3 For those in pain

Watch, dear Lord, with those who wake or weep tonight, and let your angels protect those who sleep. Tend the sick. Refresh the weary. Sustain the dying. Calm the suffering. Pity the distressed. We ask this for your love's sake. Amen.

(St Augustine of Hippo in *Commando Prayer Book*)

## 6.4 For those who suffer

Lord, we lay before you this time of crisis. In your great love, look in pity upon the wounded and prisoners; cheer the anxious; comfort the bereaved; succour the dying; have mercy on the fallen; and hasten the time when war shall cease in all the world; through Jesus Christ our Lord. Amen.          (*Pray with the Navy*)

## 6.5 For the wounded

Unto Thy loving-kindness, O Lord our God, we commend all those who are maimed and suffering through the violence of war. Bind up their wounds, O Father, and comfort them with Thy Holy Spirit, and help us all to do our part more effectually in ministering to them for the sake of Him who bore for us the pain and desolation of the Cross, even Jesus Christ our Saviour. Amen.          (*The Scottish Service Book*)

## 6.6 A Jewish prayer for healing

Heal us, Lord, and we shall be healed; save us, and we shall be saved; for it is You we praise. Send relief and healing for all our diseases, our sufferings and our wounds; for you are a merciful and faithful healer. Blessed are you, Lord, who heals the sick.

(From *Jewish Service Book* in *Pray with the Navy*)

## 6.7 When sick or wounded

O most righteous God, thou hast seen fit to lay me aside from active duty, and to appoint for me pain and suffering; may I patiently submit to thy holy will, and be kept from murmuring and repining. Thou canst heal the maladies of my body, and make the remedies employed efficacious. If it be for thy glory, may I be restored to health, and may I yet live to serve my God and my country. Grant, too, that I may be prepared for all that may happen, so that whether I live I may live to the Lord, or whether I die I may die to the Lord, and living or dying still be his. This I ask for the Saviour's sake. Amen.

*(The Soldier's Prayer Book)*

## 6.8 For the sick

Heavenly Father, giver of life and health: Comfort and relieve those who are sick, and give your power of healing to those who minister to their needs, that those for whom our prayers are offered may be strengthened in their weakness and have confidence in your loving care; through Jesus Christ our Lord, who lives and reigns with you and the Holy Spirit, one God, now and for ever. Amen.

('Prayer for the sick' from the Bible,
Naval Military and Air Force Bible Society)

## 6.9 A Jewish prayer for use with the dying

I acknowledge unto thee, O Lord my God and God of my fathers, that both my cure and my death are in thy hands. May it be thy will to send me a perfect healing. Yet if my death be fully determined by thee, I will in love accept it at thy hand. O may my death be an atonement for all the sins, iniquities and transgressions of which I have been guilty against thee. Vouchsafe unto me of the abounding happiness that is treasured up for the righteous. Make known to me the path of life: in thy presence is fulness of joy; at thy right hand are pleasures for evermore.

Thou who art the father of the fatherless and judge of the widow, protect my beloved kindred with whose soul my own is knit. Into thy hand I commend my spirit; thou hast redeemed me, O Lord God of truth. Amen, and Amen!

('Confession on a death bed' from *Prayer Book for Jewish Sailors and Soldiers*)

## 6.10 For a dying comrade

Almighty God, look on this person, lying in great weakness, and draw them to yourself in their final hours. May they experience the promise of life everlasting,

given in the resurrection of your Son Jesus Christ our
Lord. Amen.

('Prayer for the dying' from the Bible,
Naval Military and Air Force Bible Society)

## 6.11 Islamic prayers for the dying

1  Allah is great! *(repeat four times)*
2  O God, I ask of Thee a perfect faith, a sincere
   assurance, a reverent heart, a remembering tongue,
   a good conduct of commendation, and a true repentance, repentance before death, rest at death, and
   forgiveness and mercy after death, clemency at the
   reckoning, victory in paradise and escape from
   the fire, by Thy mercy, O mighty One; O Forgiver,
   Lord increase me in knowledge and join me unto
   good.
3  O Lord, may the end of my life be the best of it; may
   my closing acts be my best acts, and may the best of
   my days be the day when I shall meet Thee. Amen.

('Prayers for the dying' from *A Prayer
Book for the Armed Services*)

## 6.12 On the point of death

Go forward on your journey from this world,
   Christian soul.
In the name of God the Father who created you.

In the name of Jesus Christ who suffered for you.
In the name of the Holy Spirit who gives you
strength. Amen.
(*Armed Forces Operational Service and Prayer Book*)

## 6.13 On the death of a comrade

Give eternal rest to my colleague, O Lord,
and let perpetual light shine on *him/her*.
May *he/she* rest in peace.
May *his/her* soul and the souls of all our fallen
colleagues rest in peace. Amen.

('Death of a colleague' from *Armed Forces
Operational Service and Prayer Book*)

## 6.14 Collect for the fallen

O God the Preserver and Saviour of all men, we commit to thy holy and merciful keeping, the souls of all
who fall in this war; Grant to them we beseech thee,
a merciful judgement in the last day, that in the face
of all thy creatures they may then be acknowledged as
thy true children: through Jesus Christ our Lord. Amen.

('Collect for the Fallen, authorised by the Bishop of
London', part of an unpublished volume of collected
liturgical fragments entitled 'Services in Time of
War', compiled during the First World War by
an unknown padre in 'Army Book 136'.)

## 6.15 Prayer at the burial of the dead after a battle

O Lord God of hosts, who hast brought us in safety through the peril of battle and hast at this time called us in sorrow to commit to the dust the dead bodies of our brethren in arms who have fallen, we desire to approach Thee in prayer through Jesus Christ, the Captain of our salvation, asking Thee to enable us all to remember Thy great mercy, and the love of Christ, in whom is all our hope for this life and for the next.

Comfort, we beseech Thee, the friends and relatives of the fallen. Provide for their wants and alleviate their sorrows. Help them to bow in meek submission to Thy will. And in their bereavements draw them more closely unto Thee, who wilt never leave them nor forsake them.

We thank Thee, O God, that we have good hope that as these our brethren quitted themselves like men, and fell at last, faithful unto death, fighting for a righteous cause; so they died in faith in Christ, and now rest in peace, waiting for a blessed resurrection. And we pray that we who remain may be able to persevere in righteousness, so that, at last, having fought the good fight of faith, we may receive the crown of life, and a place in the heavenly glory.

(Church of Scotland, 1897, in *Prayers for Soldiers*)

## 6.16 When a comrade has died

Lead this, our fallen companion, by your mercy, Lord.

Comfort those of us remaining here and help us seek your kingdom till our life in this age is over, and bring us into your kingdom in the age to come.

God, the Father of all, whose Son commanded us to love one another: Lead us from prejudice to truth; deliver us from hatred, cruelty and revenge; and in your good time enable us all to stand reconciled before you; through Jesus Christ our Lord.

Almighty God, kindle, we pray, in every heart the true love of peace, and guide with your wisdom those who take counsel for the nations of the earth, that in tranquillity your dominion may increase until the earth is filled with the knowledge of your love; through Jesus Christ our Lord, who lives and reigns with you, in the unity of the Holy Spirit, one God, now and for ever. Amen.

('Prayer when a comrade has fallen' from the Bible, Naval Military and Air Force Bible Society)

## 6.17 An Orthodox prayer for the dead

Give rest, O Christ, to your servants with your saints, where sorrow and pain are no more;
neither sighing but life everlasting.
You only are immortal, the creator and maker of all:

and we are mortal, formed from the dust of the earth,
and unto earth we shall return.
For so you ordained when you created me, saying:
'Dust you are, and unto dust you shall return.'
All of us go down to the dust,
yet weeping at the grave, we make our song:
Alleluia, alleluia, alleluia!

> ('The Kontakion – a prayer for the dead' from
> *Armed Forces Operational Service and Prayer Book*)

## 6.18 A blessing at a repatriation ceremony

Go now from your Corps family, to be with your
earthly family, in the love of the heavenly family,
Father, Son and Holy Spirit.

> (Revd Stu Hallam RN at the repatriation of
> Lieutenant John 'JT' Thornton, Afghanistan,
> *Church Times*, 12 November 2010)

## 6.19 On recovering from sickness

O God, who art the giver of life, of health, and
of safety; We bless thy Name, that thou hast been
pleased to deliver from *his* bodily sickness this thy
*servant*, who now desireth to return thanks unto thee,
in the presence of all thy people. Gracious art thou,
O Lord, and full of compassion to the children of
men. May *his* heart be duly impressed with a sense

of thy merciful goodness, and may *he* devote the residue of *his* days to an humble, holy, and obedient walking before thee; through Jesus Christ our Lord. Amen.

('For a recovery from sickness' from
*A Prayer Book for Soldiers and Sailors*, 1917)

## 6.20 A prayer following trauma

Lord Jesus Christ, in the darkness of my loss I come to you; I cannot believe what has happened and yet I know that it is true. Sorrow and anxiety fill my life and it's hard to find rest. So I come to you, Lord Jesus. I bring to you the burden in my heart – it is too heavy for me; please take the weight and bear it with me, Lord, and give me your peace. Amen.

(Christian Publicity Organisation in
*Pray with the Navy*)

## 6.21 For one with troubling memories

Deliver me, God my Peace, from the dread of
   memory,
from the violence that fills my eyes and has not left
   my heart.
Lift from me distressing dreams,
regrets, doubts, and speculations.
The past is done.

Help me to lay it in your compassionate and
    forgiving hands
and to trust myself and all others to your mercy.
Let gladness and ease of heart return to me,
and let me never forget that your love for me
    endures
even when I cannot love myself. Amen.

(Jennifer Phillips, in *A Prayer Book for
the Armed Services*)

## 6.22 A reflection on praying with prisoners

I was given a posse of twenty German prisoners under
a German sergeant and all under the supervision of
two armed soldiers to do what could be done. The
prisoners were newly 'in' and were unfit to do much,
being sick as they touched the dead. I found I was
heavily involved and we dragged as many bodies
as we could to a trench where we laid them side
by side. Through their NCO, who spoke English,
I asked that any Christians among the prisoners
would raise their hands. None did. I then said I did
not mind what religion they had on their identity
discs, but would they pray with me so that, together
in German and English, we would pray the Lord's
prayer, then I would pray for peace, for all bereaved,
and for all being hurt in the conflict. A few hands

went up – to be followed by all. We marched back to the POW cage and the NCO fell his men in in front of me and gave me the only Nazi salute I ever got.

(The Very Revd Ivan D. Neill, *Far from Tipperary*)

### 6.23 For the healing of the nations

O Lord Jesus, stretch forth your wounded hands in blessing over all your people to heal and to restore, and to draw them to yourself and to one another in love. Amen.

('A Prayer of the Middle East for healing' from *Commando Prayer Book*)

### 6.24 A soldier's prayer of reflection and thanksgiving

I asked God for strength that I might achieve.
I was made weak that I might learn humbly to obey.
I asked for health that I might do great things.
I was given infirmity that I might do better things.
I asked for riches that I might be happy.
I was given poverty that I might be wise.
I asked for power that I might have the praise of men.
I was given weakness that I might feel the need of God.
I asked for all things that I might enjoy life.
I was given life that I might enjoy all things.

I got nothing that I asked for but everything I had
    hoped for.
Almost despite myself my unspoken prayers were
    answered.
I am, among all people, most richly blessed.
           (Anonymous Confederate soldier, *c.* 1865)

# 7

## *Where there is hatred, let me sow love . . .*

### Prayers of reconciliation, return and remembrance

The desire for peace is not the reserve of any one faction within the Church. All Christians are united in their calling to follow the Prince of Peace, to be peacemakers, and to work towards the creation of a peaceable kingdom. Many individuals, churches and communities have a long-standing commitment to peace activism. They have faithfully questioned the government and military when necessary, serving as the conscientious core of the Church and of the nation. Others play their part as peacemakers within the armed forces. This can take many forms – providing pastoral care and prayer support for their fellow service-men and -women, engaging in humanitarian missions or participating in peacekeeping operations.

During times of war, Christian service personnel can still work for peace, acting in accordance with the Geneva Conventions, challenging perceived illegalities and practising the core Christian values. That said, during conflict, their capacity to question the rationale behind a war is necessarily limited by their military role. It is at these times that Christians within the military become reliant upon others 'outside the wire'. We, who feel called to embody Christ's values within the dark places, can only do so, with integrity, when we are sure in the knowledge that there are others unencumbered by the constraints of uniform, who remain free to analyse the motives for war, to hold decision-makers to account, and to remind us all of the ultimate vision of God's peace established across the earth.

This Christian desire for peacemaking is not at odds with the British military mentality. A dynamic tension exists within all military personnel between two competing emotions: the desire to serve on operations – and so to do what one has trained to do – versus the desire to spend time at home, with one's loved ones, living in peace. In many cases combat seems to serve as a catalyst for the latter. Among the veterans, it is often those who have spent most time on the front line, weathering the storm, waiting patiently for the release of either ceasefire or death, who are now, in peacetime, most articulate in their calls for future military restraint. Here, it seems, the desire for peace, birthed on the battlefield, has grown strong on a diet of experience, suffering and moral incertitude.

## 7.1 For our enemies

Lord Jesus Christ, before whose judgment seat we shall all stand, we pray, as you have taught us, for our enemies; so turn their hearts and ours that we all may truly repent; and grant that they and we, being cleansed from sin, may know and do your will. For you were lifted up upon the cross to draw all people to yourself, our Saviour, our Lord and our God. Amen.

(*Armed Forces Operational Service and Prayer Book*)

## 7.2 For peace

O God, our Father, through all the clouds of war help us to see the vision of Thy peace for which we strive. Give to us self-control and steady purpose that the Kingdom which is not of this world may be established in the hearts of all men everywhere, through Jesus Christ our Lord. Amen.

(*Service Hymn Book*)

## 7.3 For our foes

Father of all, Who makest men to be of one mind in an house, forasmuch as our confusion is in ourselves and our peace is in Thee, give us the grace of under-standing, and by mutual prayer and penitence make our foes our friends, that together we may worship Thee in brotherly love through Jesus Christ our Lord. Amen.

(Father Andrew sdc, *Prayers for Use in War-Time*)

## 7.4 For an end to the war

O Almighty God, who canst bring good out of evil, and makest even the wrath of man to turn to thy praise: We beseech thee so to consider and dispose the issue of this war, that we may be brought through strife to a lasting peace; and that the nations of the world may be united in a firmer fellowship for the pro-motion of thy glory and the good of all mankind; through Jesus Christ our Lord. Amen.

(*The Army Prayer Book, India*)

## 7.5 For grace to forgive

Merciful God, in whose dear Son we have redemp-tion, even the forgiveness of sins; Give us such strong belief in this the only power that can abolish evil that

we shall be enabled to forgive our enemies; and grant
us grace not only to forgive but to accept forgiveness
through Christ, the crucified. Amen.

> (*A Prayer Book for Soldiers and Sailors*, 1941)

## 7.6 For reconciliation

O God, the Father of all, whose Son commanded us
to love our enemies: Lead them and us from prejudice
to truth; deliver them and us from hatred, cruelty,
and revenge; and in your good time enable us all to
stand reconciled before you; through Jesus Christ
our Lord. Amen.

> ('For our enemies' from *A Prayer Book for
> the Armed Services*)

## 7.7 For the journey home

O Lord our God, and God of our fathers!
Mercifully direct and guide our steps to our
    destination
and let us arrive there in health, joy and peace!
Keep us from snares and dangers
and protect us from any dangers that we may meet
    along the way.
Bless and protect our journey!
Let us win favour in your eyes
and in the sight of those around us.

Blessed are you, O Lord,
who hears and grants our prayers. Amen.

*(Pray with the Navy)*

## 7.8 For a good homecoming

In the secret spaces of our hearts
we reflect on our return home in coming days.
We think of the people we most want to see,
and the people we least want to see.
We think of the people who most want to see us,
and the people who least want to see us.
We think of our loved-ones,
and the changes we will see in them,
and the changes they may see in us.
And we pray for grace, carefulness, gentleness
and good humour enough to cope with all of it,
Through the mercy of Christ Jesus our Lord.
Amen.

*(The Naval Church Service Book, Leader's Copy)*

## 7.9 A prayer of reflection

Lord, as we remember with sadness the horrors of war,
help us to work for a better understanding between
races and nations. Open our eyes to see our own part
in discord and aggression between peoples, forgive
us our pride and divisions, and renew in us the search

for peace so that trust may replace suspicion, friendship replace fear, and your spirit of reconciliation be known among us all. Amen.

(The Revd Christian Heycocks RN in
*Commando Prayer Book*)

## 7.10 A remembrance of the fallen

Our heavenly Father, we rejoice in the blessed communion of all thy saints, wherein thou givest us also to have part. We remember before thee all who have departed this life in thy faith and love, and especially those most dear to us. We thank thee for our present fellowship with them, for our common hope, and for the promise of future joy. Oh, let the cloud of witnesses, the innumerable company of those who have gone before, and entered into rest, be to us an example of godly life, and even now may we be refreshed with their joy; so that with patience we may run the race that yet remains before us, looking unto Jesus the author and finisher of our faith.

(From *Book of Prayers*, 1851, in *A Pocket-Book
of Prayers for those on Active Service and
for those at Home*)

## 7.11 Remembrance intercessory prayers

Let us pray for all who suffer as a result of conflict, and ask that God may give us peace:

For the service men and women who have died in
   the violence of war,
each one remembered by and known to God;
May God give peace;
All: **God give peace**.

For those who love them in death as in life,
offering the distress of our grief and the sadness of
   our loss;
May God give peace;
All: **God give peace**.

For all members of the armed forces who are in
   danger this day,
remembering family, friends and all who pray for
   their safe return;
May God give peace;
All: **God give peace**.

For civilian women, children and men whose
   lives are disfigured by war or terror, calling to
   mind in penitence the anger and hatreds of
   humanity;
May God give peace;
All: **God give peace**.

For peace-makers and peace-keepers,
who seek to keep this world secure and free;

May God give peace;
All: **God give peace**.

For all who bear the burden and privilege of leadership,
political, military and religious;
asking for gifts of wisdom and resolve in the
    search for reconciliation and peace.
May God give peace;
All: **God give peace**.

O God of truth and justice,
we hold before you those whose memory we cherish,
and those whose names we will never know.
Help us to lift our eyes above the torment of this
    broken world,
and grant us the grace to pray for those who wish
    us harm.
As we honour the past,
may we put our faith in your future;
for you are the source of life and hope,
now and for ever.
All: **Amen**.

> (*Order of Service for Remembrance Sunday 2005*,
> Churches Together in Britain and Ireland)

### 7.12 In remembrance

Almighty God, who art King over all, and who in the
multitude of thy mercies hast brought us to this day,

we thank thee for all thy goodness and loving-kindness. For the gracious Providence that guided and sustained us in the dark days of the War, and for the defence thou didst raise up for us in our necessity; we give thee thanks and praise. For the grace that upheld us through the years of peril and sorrow, and for the final deliverance thou didst vouchsafe unto us; we praise and bless thy holy name. We cried unto thee in trouble, and thou didst hear us: we put our trust in thee, and were not confounded.

Grant, O Lord, we humbly beseech thee, that, we being mindful of thy great goodness, may yield ourselves in new obedience to thy holy will, and live as those who are not their own, but are bought with a price; through Jesus Christ our Lord, who liveth and reigneth and is worshipped and glorified with thee, O Father, and the Holy Spirit, one God for evermore. Amen.     (*Divine Service Book for the Armed Forces*)

## 7.13 Memorial prayer for those fallen in battle

O God, who art full of compassion, who dwellest on high, grant perfect rest beneath the shelter of thy divine presence, in the exalted places among the holy and pure who shine as of the brightness of the firmament, to all who have bravely laid down their lives for their King and Country. We beseech thee, Lord of

Compassion, shelter them for evermore under the cover of thy wings, and let their souls be bound up in the bond of eternal life. The Lord is their inheritance: may they rest in peace.

And the work of righteousness shall be peace, and the effect of righteousness quietness and confidence for ever. Nation shall not lift up sword against nation, neither shall they learn war any more. And the glory of the Lord shall be revealed, and all flesh shall see it together. Amen.

(*Prayer Book for Jewish Sailors and Soldiers*)

## 7.14 For ongoing peace in the world

God of peace,
We know we cannot bring your peace to the world
If there is no peace within and between us.
Heal whatever troubles our minds,
Whatever disturbs our hearts,
Whatever divides us from those nearest to us,
So that we may serve well those who most need to
    find God's peace, Amen.

(*The Naval Church Service Book, Leader's Copy*)

## 7.15 For peace within the British Empire

Lord, bless this Kingdom and Empire, that religion and virtue may flourish among us, that there may be peace within our gates, and prosperity in all our borders. In time of trouble guide us, and in peace may we not forget thee; and whether in plenty or in want, may all things be so ordered, that we may patiently and peaceably seek thy kingdom and its righteousness, the only full supply and sure foundation both of men and states; so that we may continue a place and people to do thee service to the end of time; through Jesus Christ our only Saviour and Redeemer. Amen.

('For the Empire' from *Divine Service Book for the Armed Forces*)

## 7.16  A Hindu prayer for peace and harmony

Let us pray in our hearts for a League of Souls and a United World. Though we may seem divided by race, creed, colour, class and political prejudices, still, as children of the one God, we are able in our souls to feel brotherhood and world unity. May we work for the creation of a United World in which every nation will be a useful part, guided by God through man's enlightened conscience. In our hearts we can all learn to be free from hate and selfishness. Let us pray for harmony among the nations, that they may march hand in hand through the gate of a fair new civilisation.

(Parmahansa Yogananda in *Pray with the Navy*)

### 7.17 For peace and peacemakers

Almighty God, inspire in the hearts of all people the true love of peace, especially in those who direct the nations of the earth. May your Holy Spirit strengthen all who strive to maintain peace and resolve conflict. May your grace be given to those who seek to build bridges between people; this we ask in the name of Jesus Christ our Lord. Amen.

(*Armed Forces Operational Service and Prayer Book*)

### 7.18 A prayer for peace

O Great Spirit,
Help me always to speak the truth quietly,
to listen with an open mind when others speak,
and to remember the peace
that may be found in silence.

('Cherokee Indian Prayer', ChaplainCare website)

### 7.19 For peaceful resolution to political conflict

We who live with the reality of war,
who must be the first to go in harm's way into battle,
we pray that we might not have to use our power
    with a vengeance.
Rather, Lord,
we ask you to help the people of our world
overcome their fears and mistrusts.

Enable them to speak and comprehend one
   another,
enough to reach an understanding
whereby all of us might enjoy the treasure
which surpasses all other treasures. Amen.

                       (*Refuge and Strength*)

## 7.20 For peace among the nations

Almighty God our heavenly Father, guide the nations
of the world into the way of justice and truth, and
establish among them that peace which is the fruit of
righteousness, that they may become the kingdom
of our Lord and Saviour Jesus Christ. Amen.

       (*A Prayer Book for the Armed Services*)

## 7.21 Prayer of St Francis

Lord, make me an instrument of your peace.
Where there is hatred, let me sow love;
Where there is injury, pardon;
Where there is doubt, faith;
Where there is despair, hope;
Where there is darkness, light;
And where there is sadness, joy.

O, Divine Master,
Grant that I may not so much seek

To be consoled as to console;
To be understood as to understand;
To be loved as to love.
For it is in giving that we receive;
It is in pardoning that we are pardoned;
It is in dying that we are born to eternal life,
Through Jesus Christ our Lord. Amen.

> (Traditional Christian prayer from
> *Pray with the Navy*)

### 7.22  For an end to warfare

O God, Who hast revealed thy purpose for mankind
in him who is King of Righteousness and Prince of
Peace; inspire the hearts of all men to follow after
justice, and hasten the time when nation shall not lift
up sword against nation, neither shall they war any
more; through Jesus Christ our Lord. Amen.

> (*Divine Service Book for the Armed Forces*)

### 7.23  For a nation committed to peace

Almighty God,
bless our Sovereign Lady Queen Elizabeth,
and all who are set in authority under her Crown:
in Parliament and in the Armed Forces.
Grant that they may order things with wisdom,
and in the spirit of reconciliation and peace;

for the good of your Church and people;
through Jesus Christ our Lord. Amen.

('For the Queen and all in authority' from
*Armed Forces Operational Service and Prayer Book*)

## 7.24 Serving, that others may live in peace

Almighty God, the origin of all love,
Let us never forget,
Amid all the trappings of our military life,
That our calling is to serve the cause of love:
To show mercy to those in need around the world,
To frustrate the plans of the wicked,
And to enable people to walk the ways of peace,
Following in the footsteps of Jesus Christ our Lord.
     Amen.

(*The Naval Church Service Book, Leader's Copy*)

# Sources and acknowledgements

## Sources

*Sources are listed in alphabetical order of volume name.*

Armed Forces' Chaplaincy Centre Archive, London: Ministry of Defence: 3.3, 3.7, 3.10, 3.15, 3.16, 3.18, 3.20, 3.26, 3.28, 3.30, 3.32, 3.34, 3.35, 3.37, 3.38, 6.14

*Armed Forces Operational Service and Prayer Book*, Portsmouth: Ministry of Defence, 2010: 1.12, 1.21, 1.38, 1.40, 3.2, 4.18, 4.25, 6.12, 6.13, 6.17, 7.1, 7.17, 7.23

*The Armed Forces Simple Prayer Book*, London: Catholic Truth Society, 2013: 1.3, 1.5, 2.9, 2.11, 2.20, 2.25, 3.14, 3.25, 3.33

*Army Prayer Book*, Oxford: Oxford University Press, 1942: 2.12

*The Army Prayer Book, India*, Delhi: Government of India Press, 1940: 1.30, 1.32, 3.23, 3.27, 4.2, 4.20, 7.4

The Bible, NIV, Naval Military and Air Force Bible Society: 6.8, 6.10, 6.16

*Catholic Prayer Book for HM Forces*, Portu-Said: Apostolicus Canalis Suezii, 1940: 4.19

United States Navy Chaplain Corps: ChaplainCare website, 2015: 1.37, 2.10, 2.27, 2.30, 7.18

Charles Walford, *The Christian Soldier's Manual of Prayer*, London: SPCK, 1900: 3.1

A. R. Howell, *Church Prayers for War-Time*, London: Oxford University Press, 1940: 5.3

*Church Times*, 12 November 2010: 6.18

M. Tobias, *Collects for the British Army*, Plymouth: Underhill, 1930: 3.4, 3.6, 3.8, 3.12, 3.13, 3.19, 3.22, 3.29

*Commando Prayer Book*, ed. Corps Chaplain, London: Ministry of Defence, 2004: 2.2, 2.15, 2.21, 4.14, 4.26, 6.3, 6.23, 7.9

*Divine Service Book for the Armed Forces*, Toronto: Canadian Council of Churches, 1950: 1.15, 1.31, 2.13, 2.22, 3.9, 3.17, 3.21, 3.36, 4.1, 7.12, 7.15, 7.22

The Very Revd Ivan D. Neill, *Far from Tipperary: An Army Chaplain's Adventure of Faith*, Uckfield: Ivan D. Neill, 2000: 6.22

*Field Service Book*, London: HMSO, 1987: 1.14, 1.16

*A Form of Prayer for Open Air Services*, London: SPCK, 1915: 3.11

*A Form of Prayer for Open Air Services*, London: SPCK, 1902: 4.35

*A Harvest of German Verse*, ed. and tr. Margarete Munsterberg, New York: D. Appleton and Co., 1916: 4.36

*The Hymnal Army and Navy*, Washington, DC: US Government Printing Office, 1941: 1.33, 1.39

*The Naval Church Service Book, Leader's Copy*, Portsmouth: Ministry of Defence, 2012: 1.18, 2.1, 4.24, 7.8, 7.14, 7.24

*The Naval Officer's Little Book of Graces*, Dartmouth: Chaplaincy Dartmouth Naval College, 2005: 2.19, 2.28

The Department of National Defence, Canada, *Order of Divine Service for the CASF*, Ottawa: J. O. Patenaude, 1940: 4.7

*Per Christum Vinces: Prayers in Time of War*, ed. Ethel M. Barton, London: Longmans, Green and Co., 1939: 5.2, 5.4, 5.7, 5.15, 5.18, 5.20, 5.26, 5.29, 5.31

*A Pocket-Book of Prayers for those on Active Service and for those at Home*, ed. Geoffrey H. Woolley, London: SCM Press, 1940: 7.10

*The Pocket Padre*, comp. H. S. Astbury and R. S. B. Sinclair, London: SCM Press, 1941: 3.5

*Prayer Book for Jewish Sailors and Soldiers*, London: HMSO, 1917: 1.28, 4.6, 5.1, 6.9, 7.13

*A Prayer Book for Soldiers and Sailors*, Philadelphia: Bishop White Prayer Book Society, 1917: 1.2, 1.19, 1.35, 2.5, 3.31, 4.3, 6.2, 6.19

The Army and Navy Commission of the Protestant Episcopal Church, *A Prayer Book for Soldiers and Sailors*, New York: The Church Pension Fund, 1941: 7.5

*A Prayer Book for the Armed Services*, New York: Church Publishing Inc., 2008: 3.24, 4.8, 4.32, 6.11, 6.21, 7.6, 7.20

*Prayers and Graces*, ed. Allan M. Laing, London: Gollanz Publishing, 1944: 4.16, 5.30

*Prayers for Men in the Armed Forces*, Fort Erie, Ontario: St George's Press, 1962: 1.11, 1.13, 1.17, 1.22, 1.27

*Prayers for Soldiers*, Edinburgh: William Blackwood and Sons, 1905: 6.15

Father Andrew sdc, *Prayers for Use in War-Time*, London: Plaistow Press, *c.* 1940: 5.9, 5.17, 5.22, 5.24, 5.25, 5.28, 7.3

*Prayers in Time of War*, ed. Hugh Martin, London: SCM Press, 1940: 5.6, 5.8, 5.16, 5.19, 5.21, 5.23, 5.27

*Pray with the Navy*, London: Ministry of Defence, 2004: 1.1, 1.4, 1.6, 1.9, 1.23, 1.34, 1.36, 2.6, 2.18, 2.24, 2.26, 2.29, 4.9, 4.11, 4.15, 4.31, 6.4, 6.6, 6.20, 7.7, 7.16, 7.21

RAF Chaplaincy website: 2.4

*Refuge and Strength: Prayers for the Military and their Families*, New York: Church Publishing Inc., 2008: 1.7, 1.8, 1.24, 1.26, 4.10, 4.23, 7.19

Church of Scotland, *The Scottish Service Book*, Oxford: Oxford University Press, 1963: 2.17, 2.23, 4.28, 6.1, 6.5

*Service Hymn Book*, Methodist and United Board, 1944: 1.25, 4.4, 4.17, 7.2

*Service Prayer Book*, Minneapolis, MN: Augsburg Publishing House, 1940: 2.8, 4.21, 4.22, 4.29, 4.33

*A Simple Prayer Book for Soldiers*, London: Catholic Truth Society, 1916: 4.5

G. R. Gleig, Chaplain-General, *The Soldier's Manual of Devotion*, London: SPCK, 1900: 4.12, 4.13, 4.27

*The Soldier's Prayer Book*, Charleston, SC: South Carolina Tract Society, 1863: 2.7, 6.7

*Some Prayers for Use in the Army Cadet Force*, Aldershot: ACFA, 1958: 1.10

*Song and Service Book for Ship and Field*, Washington, DC: United States Government Printing Office, 1942: 2.16

Chaplain Arthur Hichens, *Sunday at 09:30 Hours: Addresses on a Royal Air Force Station*, London: Epworth Press, 1944: 1.20

*They Shall Grow Not Old, Liturgies for Remembrance*, ed. Brian Elliott, Norwich: Canterbury Press, 2006: 7.11

A. Becker, *War and Faith: The Religious Imagination in France, 1914–1930*, tr. H. McPhail, Oxford: Berg, 1998: 4.30, 4.34

John Taylor Smith, Chaplain-General, *The War. Our Sailors and Soldiers: The Chaplain-General's Call for Mid-Day Prayer*, London: SPCK, 1914–18: 5.5, 5.10, 5.12, 5.14

# *Acknowledgements*

*Acknowledgements are listed in order of first entry in each acknowledgement.*

I am grateful to all the authors and publishers who have given permission for their material to be reproduced as part of this collection.

Every effort has been made to seek permission to use copyright material reproduced in this book. The publisher apologizes for those cases where permission might not have been sought and, if notified, will formally seek permission at the earliest opportunity.

Prayers 1.1 'For strength during training', 1.4 'For God's blessing during training', 1.9 'On gaining promotion', 1.34 'For family life', 1.36 'For families', 2.6 'For our ship', 2.18

'For the Royal Naval Reserve', 2.24 'For the Special Boat Service', 2.26 'For the Fleet Air Arm', 2.29 'For other sea-farers', 4.11 'For strength of character', 4.31 'In the face of fear', 6.4 'For those who suffer', and 7.7 'For the journey home' from *Pray with the Navy*, Ministry of Defence, 2004, © Crown Copyright. Reproduced under licence from the Secretary of State for Defence.

Prayers 1.7 'For meaningful service', 1.8 'For those seeking promotion', 1.26 'For revival', and 7.19 'For peaceful resolution to political conflict', used with the permission of Ted Edwards.

Prayers 1.12 'For God's gifts', 1.21 'For a stronger faith', 1.38 'An evening prayer', 1.40 'When unable to sleep', 3.2 'A Collect for the armed forces', 4.18 'For freedom and justice', 4.25 'For courage in battle', 6.12 'On the point of death', 6.13 'On the death of a comrade', 7.1 'For our enemies', 7.17 'For peace and peacemakers', and 7.23 'For a nation committed to peace', from *Armed Forces Operational Service and Prayer Book*, Ministry of Defence, c. 2010, © Crown Copyright. Reproduced under licence from the Secretary of State for Defence.

Prayers 1.14 'For inner peace', and 1.16 'For divine intervention', from *Field Service Book*, Ministry of Defence, 1987, © Crown Copyright. Reproduced under licence from the Secretary of State for Defence.

Prayers 1.18 'For courage in everyday life', 7.8 'For a good homecoming', 7.14 'For ongoing peace in the world', and 7.24 'Serving, that others may live in peace', from *The Naval*

*Sources and acknowledgements*

*Church Service Book, Leader's Copy*, Ministry of Defence, 2012, © Crown Copyright. Reproduced under licence from the Secretary of State for Defence.

Prayer 1.20 'For guarded speech', reproduced by permission of The Trustees for Methodist Church Purposes.

Prayer 2.4 'The Royal Air Force, Collect 1', from the RAF Chaplaincy Website, Ministry of Defence, 2015, © Crown Copyright. Reproduced under licence from the Secretary of State for Defence.

Prayers 2.10 'Marine Prayer', and 2.30 'A marine's prayer', used with permission of the United States Navy Chaplain Corps.

Prayers 2.15 'The Commando Prayer', 2.21 'An ecumenical Eucharistic Prayer', and 7.9 'A prayer of reflection', from *Commando Prayer Book*, Ministry of Defence, 2004, © Crown Copyright. Reproduced under licence from the Secretary of State for Defence.

Prayers 2.17 'For the Royal Air Force', 2.23 'For the Merchant Navy', 4.28 'For those going into battle', 6.1 'When the battle is over', and 6.5 'For the wounded', used with permission of the Church of Scotland.

Prayers 3.14 'A soldier's prayer for good conduct', 3.25 'For more military chaplains', and 3.33 'For the British armed forces', used with permission of the Catholic Truth Society.

Prayers 3.24 'For the US Armed Forces', 4.8 'Thanksgiving for comrades', 4.32 'For rest in the midst of turmoil', 6.11 'Islamic prayers for the dying', 6.21 'For one with troubling memories', 7.6 'For reconciliation', and 7.20 'For peace among the nations', used with the permission of The Episcopal Church, USA.

Prayers 3.30 'Collect of the Special Reconnaissance Regiment', and 3.35 'For the Counter IED Task Force', Armed Forces' Chaplaincy Centre Archive. Ministry of Defence © Crown Copyright. Reproduced under licence from the Secretary of State for Defence.

Prayer 5.1 'On the declaration of war', used with permission of the United Synagogue.

Prayer 5.3 'Giving thanks in the midst of war', from *Church Prayers for War-Time* by A. R. Howell (1940). By permission of Oxford University Press.

Prayers 5.8 'For the enemy', 5.23 'For refugees', and 5.27 'For evacuees', used with permission of SCM Press.

Prayer 5.30 'A wartime grace' originally appeared as 'A benison on wartime high tea' in Allan M. Laing (ed.), *Prayers and Graces*, London: Gollanz Publishing. Gollanz Publishing is now part of The Orion Publishing Group. All attempts at tracing the copyright holder of the work have been unsuccessful.

Prayers 6.8 'For the sick', 6.10 'For a dying comrade', and 6.16 'When a comrade has died', used with the permission of the Naval, Military and Air Force Bible Society. Adapted from the Book of Common Prayer.

Prayer 6.18 'A blessing at a repatriation ceremony', used with permission of the *Church Times* and the Revd Stu Hallam RN.

Prayer 6.20 'A prayer following trauma', used with permission of the Christian Publicity Organisation.

Prayer 7.11 'Remembrance intercessory prayers', used with the permission of Churches Together in Britain and Ireland.

# Did you know that SPCK is a registered charity?

As well as publishing great books by leading Christian authors, we also . . .

. . . **make assemblies meaningful and fun for over a million children** by running www.assemblies.org.uk, a popular website that provides free assembly scripts for teachers. For many children, school assembly is the only contact they have with Christian faith and culture, and the only time in their week for spiritual reflection.

. . . **help prisoners to become confident readers** with our easy-to-read stories. Poor literacy is a huge barrier to rehabilitation. Prisoners identify with the believable heroes of our gritty fiction. At the same time, questions at the end of each chapter help them to examine their choices from a moral perspective and to build their reading confidence.

. . . **support student ministers overseas in their training**. We give them free, specially written theology books, the International Study Guides. These books really do make a difference, not just to students but to ministers and, through them, to a whole community.

Please support these great schemes: visit www.spck.org.uk/support-us to find out more.

Printed and bound by CPI Group (UK) Ltd, Croydon, CR0 4YY

09/11/2023

08186132-0001